TIME TO PLAY

MICHAEL JOSEPH · LONDON

TIME TO PLAY

*Games and Activities for Development and
Fun for Babies and Young Children*

JANE ASHER AND
DOROTHY EINON

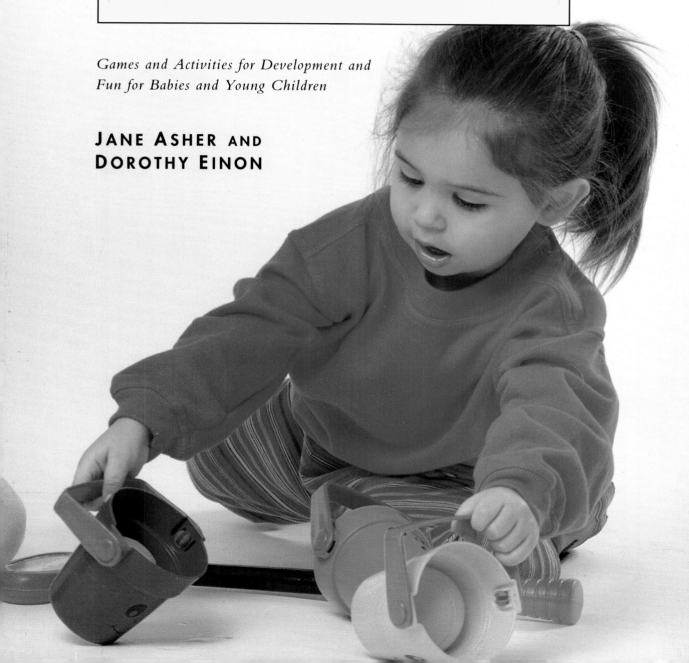

To Rory, who can play imagining games
better than anyone I know

MICHAEL JOSEPH LTD

Published by the Penguin Group
27 Wrights Lane, London W8 5TZ
Viking Penguin Inc., 375 Hudson Street, New York, New York 10014, USA
Penguin Books Australia Ltd, Ringwood, Victoria, Australia
Penguin Books Canada Ltd, 10 Alcorn Avenue, Toronto, Ontario, Canada M4V 3B2
Penguin Books (NZ) Ltd, 182–190 Wairau Road, Auckland 10, New Zealand
Penguin Books Ltd, Registered Offices: Harmondsworth, Middlesex, England

First published in Great Britain 1995

Copyright © Jane Asher and Dorothy Einon 1995

Photographs by Ray Moller
Illustrations by Gary Wing

Typeset by Cambridge Photosetting Services
Colour reproduction by Anglia Graphics, Bedford
Printed and bound in Hong Kong by Imago Publishing Limited

ISBN 0 7181 3731 0

The moral right of the authors has been asserted

CONTENTS

ACKNOWLEDGEMENTS

I am very grateful to Roger Houghton, who first asked me to write this book, to Arianne Burnette who did some magnificent text-sorting and clarifying, and to Louise Haines who stuck with it and gave me enormous support and encouragement. May they too always have time to play.

INTRODUCTION

One of the most charming sights in the animal kingdom is that of young creatures playing. From lion cubs to kittens, from baby elephants to puppies, the instinct to wrestle, tease and generally rush about just for the sheer pleasure of it seems to be something most types of animal are born with. In humans this instinct seems to be particularly marked – and particularly necessary – and we have extended the boundaries of play immeasurably by using our imaginations. Everyone knows the fascination of watching a child turn a cardboard box into a train, or a small piece of plastic into a lethal weapon of destruction just by using his imagination. We learn much about the world around us and about our own potential by projecting ourselves into pretend situations and coping with them.

Playing may be a natural instinct but that doesn't mean it never needs encouraging. A child deprived of toys and company may well amuse himself by twiddling the fringe on the carpet or making shapes with his fingers, but by limiting his opportunities his capacity to make the most of his life may well be limited too.

Some of the happiest moments of my life have been spent playing with my children, and I have tried to pass on some of the games that I found to be the most enjoyable and successful. And although it must never be a subject treated with reverence or over seriously, I think it can be helpful to know just when you can encourage the development of certain skills while at the same time having a thoroughly good time. Also, I've tried to suggest certain safe and absorbing games for each age group that the baby or child can play by himself – I don't promise any magic, but some of them just might give you five minutes with your feet up, or a chance to catch up with those thousand and one things that get neglected when a demanding young person enters your life.

I have divided the book very roughly into age groups, but as children develop at their own pace it was obviously important not to be too specific. Only you will know at exactly what age your child will be ready for certain activities, and indeed many of the games cross age barriers in any case. The sections may be useful as a guide, but it's certainly worth exploring all of the chapters for ideas.

The best games of all to play with a young child are those that you discover for yourselves – the silly, special family games that mean nothing to an outsider but which have a particular pleasure for those involved. (The game I most remember playing when I was very small was having to walk around bent almost double for most of the day being a 'teazle', a strange, speechless creature who was kept in captivity by my brother.)

I'd love to say that imaginary games are always enough. Unfortunately, my three children are as desperate to have the latest expensive toys as their friends are, and we've been through all the stages of large plastic chimney pots, dolls, fighting men from strange galaxies, turtles (of course), plastic ponies, helmets and shields (I have a photograph of which I am particularly fond of a Viking with a dummy clenched securely in his mouth) right up to the present day's computer games. Budgets allowing, I don't see any point in trying to forbid them as they give such enormous pleasure, and I can just remember from my own childhood how much it matters that you have an example of the most recent craze. But it is fun to try home-made alternatives as well, and to create a few games that don't depend on having the necessary kit.

I have very much enjoyed writing this book. Dorothy Einon and I have worked together as a team, and I have learnt a great deal from her about the psychological and developmental aspects of playing. Apart from her invaluable help and advice throughout the text, she has written paragraphs which point out any particular educational or psychological aspect of a game or activity, or which just throw interesting light on a particular stage of development. These are inset within dotted lines. I do hope you find the book helpful and that you and your baby – or babies! – will have many happy hours of playing together now and in the future.

Jane Asher

SPECIAL NEEDS

All children have difficulties in communication and/or motivation, but the degree of difficulty varies. With some children it will always be up to you to lead in play, to motivate and encourage them. Notes throughout indicate games especially suitable for children with special needs and show how to play them.

If your child cannot use one of his senses to locate people and objects, it will be important to exaggerate colour or contrast, sound or movement to make it possible for him to use any residual ability he might have. It will also be important to find ways of keeping objects within feeling distance.

For a child with visual problems, try to determine whether bright lights or dim help him most. Keep things large, and watch to see if a strong contrast between a moving object and a background interests him.

For a child who is deaf, notice if he responds to vibrations and high or low sounds. Remember smell: wear perfume and add some to his toys (change it often, as after a while we adapt to one smell).

If the child has little motor control, move his arms, legs and hands, and attach bells and smells to them.

If your child has been traumatized at birth, there may be too many problems in the first months for him to pay much attention to the world around him. It will take time for him to get over the acute effects of the trauma. He will be slow to uncurl and show much interest. This can make things especially hard for you. When we look and smile at people, we expect them to acknowledge us and to reciprocate the pleasure that we show in seeing them. It is difficult to continue talking to someone who shows no response. You may even find it is difficult to express love without the reflection of your love in his eyes. However, in time he will find ways to acknowledge you, and you will come to recognize his particular signs.

One of the needs many of these special children share is someone to help them to motivate themselves. Draw your child into games, but allow him control. Let him say no or call a halt. Show your confidence in him and let him know you believe he can do it. It is not your pity he needs but your strength and faith. However little he can do, let him do it. Only by trying will he succeed. He has to be tough if he is to become independent.

Dorothy Einon

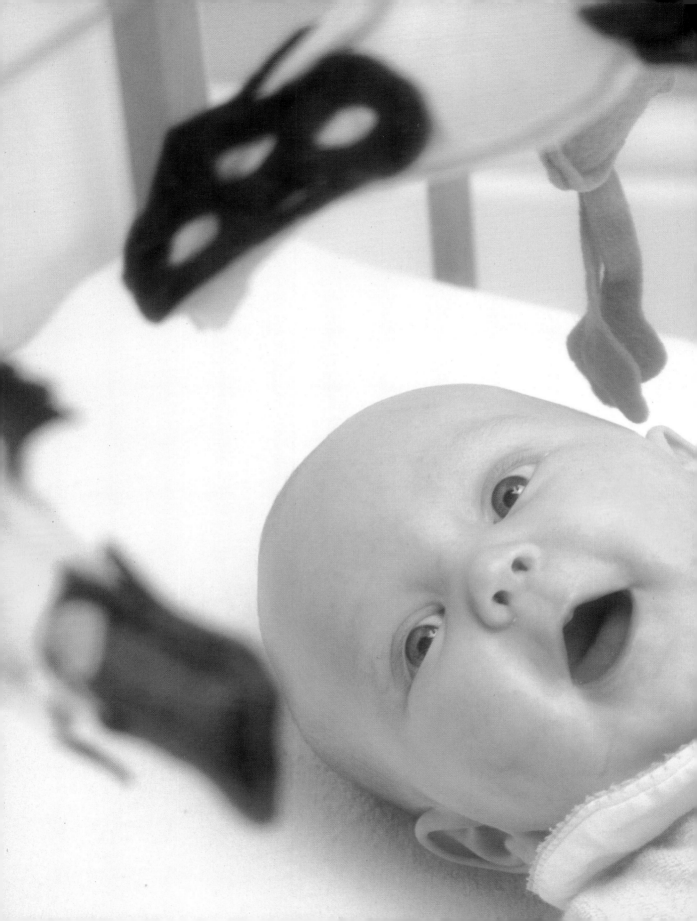

NEW
BABY

INTRODUCTION

Having a baby is such an overwhelming, extraordinary, exhausting and wonderful event that you may rightly feel that the idea of planning any sort of play with the new arrival is the last thing you should be considering. Certainly, after the birth of each of my children, I found it a full-time job just to feed, change and look after them – getting *myself* dressed in the mornings was a major challenge.

Nevertheless you *are* playing with your baby from the first moment he arrives. The instinct to tickle and coo, rub noses and use funny voices is very strong, and most parents find they have special little 'games' they play with their babies from a very early age. Almost everything you do with your baby – from bathing or nappy-changing to feeding – will naturally be done in a playful way. So you don't need to plan a baby's play time: it happens whenever you are near him.

Your baby is learning whenever he is awake, even during those sleepless nights with the inevitable crying sessions. The games I've suggested below are for times, perhaps, when the baby seems fractious or when you want to do something a bit different that will also help to develop his sensory skills. Don't ever feel that any of them is essential – a big hug and kiss are worth all the games put together.

Because you love him, you are aware of your child's needs and respond to his reactions when you play with him. You watch to see if he is interested in a game and you stop if he looks unhappy. He knows what he likes, and looking away and crying are the only ways he can say 'I don't want to play at the moment'. Respect his views, but remember he may also be trying to tell you that he is hungry, thirsty or uncomfortable. It seems natural to play like this, so you can be pretty sure you've got it right. His enjoyment tells you that you are playing the game he needs, the way he wants to and at just the right pace.

It is extraordinary the lengths a parent will go to for the reward of a smile – there is little later in life that gives you quite the same glow of pleasure as those first few wobbly, crooked grins. There would be times with our first baby when I would spend hours doing the most ludicrous things and making the silliest noises, all to no avail, and then a complete stranger would walk in and get a real dazzler for doing nothing. I used to feel quite offended.

At this stage your baby is a bit like a fuzzy television set. As he needs to understand the world around him, he will start to tune himself in. He begins with the 'Where?' channel. By watching and listening, he discovers where voices come from, where to find a face and how to follow it across a room. Babies are born with an intense desire to be social. Already he can tell the difference between language and all other sounds, and is tuned into its rhythms. Within days he will know you by your smell and, soon after, by your voice. Within weeks he will know your face.

When he is about three or four months of age, he starts to tune into the next − 'What is it?' − channel. He grabs, chews and sucks his way through everything in reach. His love of people knows no bounds, and he starts 'gurgle and smile' conversations with everyone who will answer him.

GAMES TO PLAY WITH A NEW BABY

Seeing

At first babies cannot focus. They see best at a distance of about 25–30 centimetres (10–12 inches), and beyond that everything is blurry. It is worth remembering this when you show your baby things or arrange toys for him to look at; for instance, a mobile hanging from the ceiling may look pretty to you, but it will be of no interest to your new-born baby.

By the time he is two or three weeks old, a baby can focus better, but his vision is still not the same as an adult's. To get an idea of what he can see, look around a room lit only by a street lamp outside. You can see the outlines of shapes, but no detail or colour. Movement is important: you might see the cat only when it darts across the room; likewise, your baby will be able to see things more easily if they move.

A baby views everything around him as a substitute for you, so it follows naturally that the things he likes best move, make noise and are very close.

The general rule for young babies is to exaggerate – make things big, bold, close, colourful or mobile.

Almost everything a new baby needs to know he learns from the people around him. One of his first lessons is how to interact socially, by responding with and imitating facial expressions and movement. He also learns that we continue to be the same people from whatever angle he views us, and later that we are the same people every time he sees us (before he is five months old we are new to him every morning!).

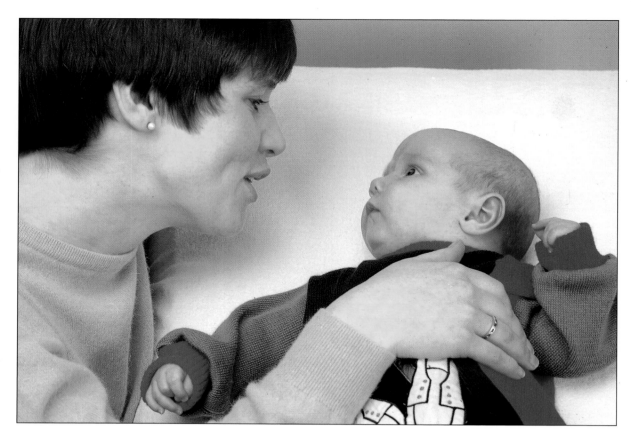

WATCHING PEOPLE •   When your baby wakes, it is natural for you to come in closer, ask him how he is and move your head. Once he begins to look around him, make it easy for him to find you. Stand right in front of him and call his name. When he is a few weeks old, you will be able to call him from the side and he will turn his head to try to find you. Help him by moving into his line of vision as soon as he starts to turn. At first his eyes will not move with his head; this exercise helps strengthen his head–eye co-ordination.

PULLING FACES • Babies at a very young age try to copy the things they see, and imitation becomes a useful learning tool as they grow older. Stick out your tongue, then pause. Your baby may try to do it himself. Open your mouth wide and look surprised, or scrunch up your face. At the very least you may get a smile.

SHOW • When you show things to your baby, remember to hold toys directly in front of his face, and move them to attract his attention. You are trying to develop his ability to fixate on an object and to follow its movement, so be sure to allow him time to focus – don't rush him. Most ceilings are white, so he may find it easier to see dark things above him, but

I don't think it is worth buying a new black wardrobe to accommodate him – he will soon find your face, which is the bit that matters to him.

Try showing him woolly pompoms, big wooden beads, balloons, bubbles, bright curtains and anything that is black and white or shiny.

Hearing

Rules similar to those for helping a baby get used to his visual surroundings also apply to the world of sound. Never frighten him with noises that are too loud or sudden, but do exaggerate a little. You may find certain sounds seem to soothe him (my second baby loved the vacuum cleaner), while others irritate him. Certainly you want him to grow up with as much normal noise and toing and froing as possible – you don't want him to get so used to silence that you have to tiptoe around the house for the next fifteen years.

When she was a very small baby, my daughter was given a T-shirt with 'Talk to me' printed on it. While it made people smile, it also got them chatting to her. Adults can feel rather foolish addressing a little baby, but almost nothing could be more important. Talk, talk, talk to your baby about anything and everything. Babies love the sound of the human voice and it is worth remembering that if they never heard anyone speak, they would grow up with no words at all. The way they learn is from copying what they hear.

Singing to a baby is even better. They say babies who are sung to regularly learn to read faster than others (perhaps just so they can bury themselves in a book and get away from that awful noise). Singing can be lovely, soothing and comforting, and has calmed babies since the dawn of man. It doesn't matter whether you can sing in tune, what the words are or what type of song it is, the gentle rocking rhythm of your voice will do the trick. It is wise to remember that a calm baby can play and learn; a tense and fearful one cannot.

> From birth your baby can find a voice if it is directly in front of him and will respond to the rhythm of your speech, but it takes practice to learn to locate you if you are off to one side. Hearing games involving conversations, rattles and music are fundamentally social, but they also encourage a baby's ability to discriminate between sounds and improve his understanding of cause and effect by teaching him that he can produce sounds too. His hearing is in a higher range than ours, which is why you instinctively raise your voice a tone or two when you speak to him.

TAKING TURNS • Conversations with a tiny baby might sound very silly to a third party, but you will know from the fascinated, intensely concentrated expression on his face that he really is trying to understand, and very soon the pauses on your side will be filled with answers. Watch him when he is about ten days old and you will see his mouth begin to move. Later he will smile, gurgle and kick his legs. It really doesn't matter what you talk about: if he is in the right mood, you will get an extremely interested response.

Good morning, darling.
Pause
How are you today?
Pause
Did you have a nice sleep?
Gurgle
What do you think about the current state of the Exchange Rate Mechanism?
Kick kick gurgle coo.

And there you have it – your first conversation.

SHAKE, RATTLE AND ROLL ● Rattles must be noisy, colourful, well-balanced and easy to hold: dumb-bells and other 'waisted' shapes are good to hang on to. They must also be safe, which means beads must not fall out, there should be no sharp edges and handles must be too wide to be pushed down the baby's throat. All rattles sold by good toy shops have to pass stringent safety checks.

You can make a variety of rattles at home using plastic screw-top jars and bottles filled with a little rice, small grains or fish grit. Glue the lids securely in place and tape them up for good measure.

MUSIC MUSIC MUSIC ● Turn on the radio. Put in a cassette. Anything will do: music to clap to, music to relax with, music to sing along with, music to dance around the room to. And, of course, there is also the music of birds and the rustling of the trees.

GAMES A NEW BABY CAN PLAY ALONE

A new baby must never be left completely alone. You must always be within earshot, even if he is safely in his cot; if he is out of his cot, you will need to be able to see him all the time as well. Nevertheless there are activities that may absorb his attention without your having to stand over him, so you can make that desperate attempt to catch up with the housework or your correspondence, or even to indulge in a cup of tea with your feet up.

Seeing

Providing various forms of visual stimulation helps a new baby to focus and co-ordinate, and bring together information from both eyes so that he can start to form a picture of the world and begin to understand the relationship between objects or between one place and another. He learns to follow an object as it moves and where to look to find it again. He looks back and forth between objects as if he is painting the spaces in between. As he plays he also learns where he stops and the rest of the world begins: for example, these are his hands and those are yours. Once he knows this he can begin to reach out.

MOBILES • If young babies are to see mobiles, they need to be mounted on the side of the cot or suspended at cot height. Be very careful – long pieces of thread or string can be dangerous; they must be too short to go around the baby's neck. It is best to fix the mobile to the ceiling on a lightweight plastic chain or a piece of plastic tubing, or to suspend the mobile from a rod fixed across the cot. Remember that a baby can see no further than an arm's length, and that he is usually looking from below. Very often mobiles can look quite boring from this angle, so find one where the pieces float horizontally. Mobiles are much more interesting if they move, so in warm weather open a window or switch on a fan nearby.

HANGING TOYS • You can suspend or tie colourful objects in a baby's line of vision wherever he happens to be lying. Just make sure that the objects are safely fixed so that there is no danger of anything falling on top of him. Always remember that babies get smarter all the time: keep checking that those things he can touch are safe, and that anything he shouldn't grab is well out of reach.

Things to look at that are out of reach:

Paper streamers
A bunch of short coloured ribbons tied together at one end and bells, buttons and shiny sequins sewn securely to the loose ends
Tinsel and other Christmas decorations
Yoghurt pots, plastic bottle tops, polystyrene cups, corks, buttons, little bells – anything bright, blunt and light.

Things to reach out and touch:

Cotton reels painted in safe, bright colours and suspended in a long line
Rattles, squeakers, furry friends and other cot toys
Safe kitchen utensils, such as wooden or plastic spoons
Small plastic mirrors (available from pet shops).

LET IT MOVE •   Babies love movement. When he is lying safely in his basket, pram or carrycot, put your baby where he can see:

Trees in the wind
Washing on the line (if you've had time to do any)
Dust in a sunbeam
Cars passing the window
Curtains blowing.

When he is a little older – and strapped in if necessary! – let him watch:

Children playing
Trains rushing through the station (this can be a little frightening at first, but it soon became one of my children's favourite sights)
Rooks flying in to roost
Television (this too, inevitably, soon became one of my children's favourite sights!).

Tricks of Light

A mirror has everything a baby needs visually: it is bright and shiny, and shows lots of movement. Thin aluminium mirrors are the safest. Either sew them into a cloth frame, making sure there are no sharp corners, or buy some of the special baby mirrors that are available.

A SECRET MIRROR TABLE★ • Stick a few mirror tiles firmly to the underside of a low table and place the baby under it so he can look up into the mirrors. Check that he has enough light to see himself. If he is dressed in pale colours, put him on a dark sheet or blanket to emphasize the contrast.

A MIRROR BALL • Make a mobile using corks covered with foil, mirrored Christmas decorations, mirror tiles stuck back to back, and so on. Hang it where it will catch the sunlight, or focus a spotlight on it when it is dark and let the baby watch the pretty reflections that will be thrown all over the walls and surfaces. It is rather 'show-biz', but very absorbing.

Hearing

If your baby can hear you pottering around while he is lying in his cot or basket, he will feel secure and calm. Some babies become very uneasy in complete silence. There are also special sounds that you can fix for him to hear which he will find fascinating.

> In the early weeks a baby's hearing is much better than his vision. Sounds help him to locate things in the hazy world around him and make it easier to follow them as they move, disappear and reappear. Putting bells on his wrists and ankles helps him not only to find his hands but also to understand that when he moves he makes something happen – he must be able to do both in order to reach for things.

SINGING BAMBOO • Hollow bamboo makes a lovely noise. If you cannot manage to hang it in a tree, then a washing line or somewhere above the bath will do – bamboo has the great advantage of being water- and

★ Any of these things would be good to do with an older child who cannot sit but has some degree of limb movement.

steam-proof. Buy a few bamboo canes – of different widths if possible –
from a garden centre, and cut them into various lengths, making the cuts
about 1 centimetre (⅜inch) above the joint. Clean the pith from the inside
of each piece using a skewer or knitting needle, and drill a small hole
through the joint. Pass a string through the hole, pull it up through the top
of the bamboo piece and tie a large knot. Pull the knot back into the bamboo
and repeat with the remaining pieces. Attach six to ten sections of bamboo
to a branch, coat hanger or a wooden aviary perch (from a pet shop). The
bamboo will make a marvellous sound as the wind – or a small hand or foot
– makes the pieces bump together.

LET ME LISTEN   •   Babies like to listen to:

Bells – because they like high notes
Rhythms – it is sometimes said that a regular rhythm reminds the baby
of his mother's heartbeat inside the womb; whatever the reason, there
is no doubt that it can be very soothing
Music – musical boxes or the radio
Voices – again, switch on the radio and let him listen to *The World at
One.*

BELLS ON HIS FINGERS AND TOES   •

Hang a few empty drinks cans (with no sharp bits) near the baby's feet
and let him kick

Fill the end of his cot with crumpled paper which rustles as he kicks
If you can find a little squeaker, sew it into one bootee and let him kick
against a solid base
Sew a few bells or squeakers safely to his mittens or, better still, tie
them round his wrists so he can wiggle his fingers. ★

★ This is especially good for helping children with special needs find their limbs, and encourages them to watch their hands.

SOCIAL BABY

INTRODUCTION

Now your baby is really displaying his own personality and fast developing into a unique individual. He smiles, gurgles and coos – and screams! – at everyone he meets. Many of the character traits that will belong to him as an adult can be seen in him now, and it is fascinating just how much seems to be 'programmed' from such an early age.

When we were very tiny, my father wrote a short description of the types of people he thought my brother, sister and I would grow into, and it was extraordinarily accurate.

Playing with your baby becomes more and more fun as he grows older. At this stage, he begins to let you know what his favourite games are and how he wants to play them.

> Gradually, your child realizes that he cannot treat everything and everyone in the same way and he tunes into his third channel, 'How can I?' He pokes and prods, picks up, drops and passes things from hand to hand – he is testing what he can do. He also anticipates, and has learned how to manipulate you effectively. By now he will have begun to talk, to coo and babble in answer to your questions. Watch carefully and you may 'see' his first 'words'. Between six and nine months he becomes more selective. His smiles are now for those he knows. His family is special to him, and he will beam with delight when he sees you.

GAMES TO PLAY WITH A SOCIAL BABY

Feeling and Exploring

Once a baby can touch his fingers with his thumb (the talent that separates us from most animals), he starts to explore objects with his hands. His mouth is still used extensively for testing, of course, but now he can roll things between his fingers and thumb, and use his forefinger to poke and prod interesting objects. A favourite game is for you to put on a hat and encourage him to pull it off – although, I must warn you, this may mean you can never wear a hat again, unless you are happy to have it removed forty-five times before you go out.

Over the next few months your child will improve his hand–eye co-ordination, learn to pick up and hold big and small objects, and polish up his ability to work his hands together and independently. He will hold things for long periods and will pass objects between his two hands; he will start purposefully to let go, put down and move objects from one place to another.

USING BOTH HANDS   •   If you sit your baby up with his legs apart and roll a ball towards him, he will try to reach for it with both hands (soft foam balls are lovely for him to play with at this age). Offer him things that are too big to hold in one hand and he will soon learn to use two.

PASSING   •   An interesting possibility will occur to your child at about this time: he can hold something in one hand while picking up a second

object with the other. He has discovered an in-built temporary storage system; instead of dropping one toy as he reaches to pick up another, he retains the first one in his spare hand. You can encourage this useful ability by offering him toys that are small enough to hold in one hand, or by giving him a bucket or bag to hold while doing something else with his free hand.

POINTING • When you come to think about it, the idea of pointing at something is quite a complex one. To expect someone to follow an imaginary line from the end of your finger to a particular object demands an extraordinary feat of lateral thinking. Yet a baby as young as nine months begins not only to understand this trick, but also to employ it himself. Make sure you point at pictures in books, at dogs in the street and even at yourself. Your child will soon start to copy you, and may well say his first word as he points.

STROKING AND SQUEEZING • At about the same time that the baby starts to poke and prod, he also enjoys patting and stroking different textures. Let him stroke and squeeze bits of fake fur, tissue paper, smooth stones, cornflakes, a wet sponge, playdough – even mashed potato! Just make sure you pick a time when you are in the right mood for a good bit of clearing up.

Babies of this age can sometimes be allowed to stroke a docile cat or other domesticated animal gently, but do make sure that you hold the animal and that she can be trusted; you have to be ready to jump in at the slightest sign of irritation on either side. Try to put yourself in the animal's place: if a small, noisy person had recently been introduced into my household without anyone consulting me and started stroking my hair backwards after I had spent hours grooming, it might well be enough to make me lose my temper, and if my only way of saying 'enough' was to scratch or bite, I'm sure I would be tempted to do so.

SOCIAL DROPSY • A magic discovery! He has power over you. By chance one day your child comes across a game beloved of all babies – and dreaded by all parents. It goes like this: he throws his spoon on the floor. *You pick it up!!!* He throws it down again, and laughs. You pick it up, smiling. He throws it down again, laughing even more. You pick it up again, smiling a little less. And so on, *ad infinitum*, until one of you tires of this enthralling exchange. But at least you don't scream until you are blue in the face when he tires of it, whereas the other way round...

Variations on the theme include:

Throwing the toys out of the pram
Dropping the dinner from the high chair (this is particularly satisfying for one of the players)

Pouring bath water over the side (as above)
Throwing shopping out of the trolley.
You may wish to discourage some of these interesting versions of the game.

Communication

By now your child knows he can make things happen. His greatest successes come from manipulating people. He is becoming more aware of the connection between words and objects or actions. For instance, 'more' is not a word he can say yet, but he has ways of letting you know that is what he wants. The slight pauses before you lift him up or offer him food teach him to anticipate and communicate his 'please'. By repeating specific words and actions, you can help to develop his memory as well.

LET ME RIDE • My children have all loved 'This is the way the ladies ride', and I can just remember my father playing it with me when I was little. It is very old-fashioned, snobbish and 'politically incorrect', and has almost nothing to do with life in the 1990s (think how few children will ever sit astride a horse), but it seems to have a timeless appeal.

You can play this as soon as the baby holds his head up firmly and smiles at you. This type of game is good for his sense of balance and his ability to anticipate. Sit the child astride your knee, facing you. Hold him firmly round the waist, and recite the following:

This is the way the ladies ride:
Trit-trot, trit-trot, trit-trot
Jog him neatly up and down on your knee
This is the way the gentlemen ride:
Gallupy, gallupy, gallupy
Jog him faster
This is the way the farmer rides:
Lollopy, lollopy, lollopy
Jog him unevenly and to the sides
This is the way the huntsman rides:
Hobbledy, hobbledy, hobbledy,
hobbledy DOWN IN THE DITCH!!
Jog him up, down and sideways,
and let him 'fall' between your knees.

The older he gets, the faster and more wildly you can jog him about. I still play this on occasion with my nine-year-old, and I end up feeling quite battered.

The actions and the ride to 'Humpty Dumpty' are obvious and you will have great fun playing this lovely old favourite with your baby:

> *Humpty Dumpty sat on a wall*
> *Humpty Dumpty had a great fall;*
> *All the king's horses,*
> *And all the king's men,*
> *Couldn't put Humpty together again.*

Listening to rhymes such as this is likely to help your child with his speaking and, eventually, with reading. The repetition of sounds and words is important, as is the recognition of slight variations, such as that between 'Humpty' and 'Dumpty'.

WORDS IN ACTIONS   •

> *Pat-a-cake, pat-a-cake, baker's man*
> *Bake me a cake as fast as you can;*
> *Pat it and prick it, and mark it with 'B',*
> *And put it in the oven for Baby and me.*

Sit facing the baby and clap your hands together first and then against his while you sing the song, or mime the making of a cake.

It always worried me that the last line of this verse didn't scan very satisfactorily but, considering a line of business I've taken up in recent years, I'm all for impressing on babies the importance of celebration cakes.

A song with actions can help a baby's understanding, as the first words are not the ones he says but the ones he signs. Deaf babies can be taught sign language at about seven months – long before hearing babies learn to speak. His early signs often come from this sort of action song. He also develops special signs to tell you he wants something from you, such as:

Pointing means 'look'
Raising his arms means 'pick me up'
Turning his head away means 'no'

Flailing his arms, turning puce and gnashing his gums means 'I SAID NO!!'

You will soon learn to recognize your baby's individual signs.

TOYS WITH MEANING •

A teddy that always tickles his tummy
An owl that always says goodnight
A doll that goes cuddle, cuddle
A car that goes 'brrmm brrmm'.

In time the regular pattern between seeing the toy and waiting for the action is understood by the baby. He will remember what each toy does and will encourage you to start the game by using the action. Pushing up his tummy for a tickle from teddy says, as clearly as words do, exactly what he wants.

TICKLE ME • Developmental psychologists have made some grand observations about tickling and the role it plays in social understanding. They need not concern us, but it is worth noting that tickles are social. (Have you ever tried to tickle yourself? It is remarkably unfunny.) Even more important, children *love* them.

Tickling with your fingers is wonderful, so is putting your mouth on his tummy and blowing a loud raspberry
Make a tickle brush from a strip of paper: fold it in half, snip a fringe along one edge, roll it up tightly, tape the handle and open out the 'brush'
Use a soft shaving brush or a large make-up brush.

'Piggies' is an old favourite, and one that becomes more and more fun as the baby gets to know it and waits in delighted fearful anticipation for the unbearable punchline. Start with the big toe and work your way across to the smallest one:

This little piggy went to market,
This little piggy stayed at home,
This little piggy had roast beef,

This little piggy had none,
And this little piggy. . .
Hold it. . .wait for it. . .
Went wee-wee-wee all the way home!
And run your hand up his body to find the most ticklish spot.

This lovely game is predictable, recognizable and your baby will soon be thrusting his foot out for more.

'Round and round the garden' is based on the 'little piggy' principle: waiting for the tickle at the end is all the fun. Why it should be thought typical of a teddy bear to walk round and round a garden I have never discovered. Some interesting research could be carried out and a thesis written on the probability of early twentieth-century teddy bears having had one leg shorter than the other, thus causing them to walk round in circles.

Hold the baby's hand in yours
Round and round the garden,
Describe a circle on his palm with your free hand
Like a teddy bear,
Keep circling
One step, two step,
Make your fingers 'walk' up his hand and on to his arm
Tickle him under there!
Give him a good tickle under his arm.

FIRST WORDS • Naturally, it is extremely exciting when your baby first starts to make recognizable words, but you mustn't panic if it is later than the baby next door. When your mother-in-law insists that your husband spoke in perfect sentences by the age of eight months, do remember to take it with a pinch of salt. They say Einstein didn't speak until he was two.

My children started 'speaking' with animal noises. One of my party tricks was to ask 'How does the dog go?', and I nearly burst with pride when my baby barked back convincingly. We quickly built up a large repertoire and I squirm now when I think how many friends I entertained with a very long performance of baas, grunts, moos and clucks.

There is a wonderful stage when a baby develops several mysterious words that only his parents understand. My second child developed a large vocabulary of his own, including 'ossedy' for water, 'danones' for television and 'oggly oggly oggly etc etc' – this word could last for some time – for coffee. The best words of all, and the ones that convince you beyond all possible doubt that you have the most wonderful, intelligent, lovable baby in the world, are: 'Mama' and 'Dada'.

BLOW★ • In order to speak children have to learn to control their breathing. Puff out your cheeks and blow at your baby; if you blow in short puffs, he will find it easier to copy you. Try putting a tissue over his face or a feather in your hand and let him blow it away. Can he blow a ping-pong ball off the edge of the table? When he has mastered the technique, he can practise blowing out candles, blowing and sucking through straws, tooting whistles, fogging up a cold window or propelling paper boats across a bowl of water.

MORNING COFFEE • This could also be afternoon tea, or even an early evening glass of wine – the choice is yours – while your child has milk or juice and a biscuit. The point is not what you drink, but that you begin

★ Deaf children and children who have speech difficulties may find blowing games useful for overcoming breathing problems.

the habit of sitting down together to discuss the day. Games can teach the basics, books can expand his vocabulary, but only talking to him can teach him the gentle art of conversation. Later you can use this time to air problems and reach compromises. Democracy, like charity, begins at home.

Hiding

Children love to hide. I've spent hours looking for one of my children when arms, legs and nappy-clad bottom were all clearly in view sticking out from behind the sofa. You can play hide-and-seek for hours, and the joy at this stage is that you don't have to keep thinking of new places: even if a child has hidden behind the sofa twelve times that morning, he will be convinced you haven't a clue where he might be on the thirteenth.

It goes without question, as far as your baby is concerned, that he continues to exist, even when he is asleep upstairs, but it is not so obvious to him that while he is asleep upstairs you continue to exist downstairs. This is something he has to learn and is one of the reasons for playing hide-and-seek games.

PEEK-A-BOO   •   This game starts when the baby is very small. You simply cover your face with your hands, wait a few seconds, then uncover

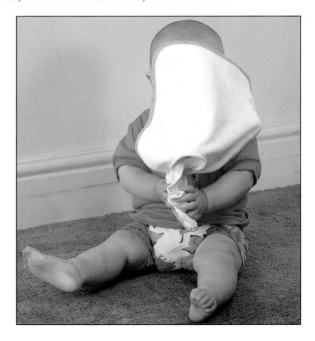

it while saying 'Boo!'. The more sophisticated versions can follow when he is a little older:

He looks
You hide behind the end of the bed
You wait; he waits
You pop up and say *'Boo!'*

You get down
You put on a hat
You pop up and say *'Boo!'*

You crawl behind the sofa
He waits
You crawl out at the other side and say *'Boo!'*

You put a sheet over his face
He pulls it off
'Boo!'

You pull his jumper on to his head, over his face
Where's Jamie?
You pull it down over his head
There he is!

POP-UP TOYS • A Jack-in-the-box is another sort of peek-a-boo. You can buy one, but an instant substitute can be made from the top half of a washing-up liquid container and an old-fashioned dish mop. You could even add a face to the mop by sticking on a couple of buttons and a red paper smile. Turn the container upside-down and pull the mop handle down through the neck so that the mop top is hidden inside. Push up the mop and say 'Boo!'.

To make a pop-up doll, use a large plastic bottle with the bottom cut off or make a cone of strong cardboard. Paint it and let it dry. Paint a face on the back of a wooden spoon (make sure the handle will fit through the neck of the bottle). Add some wool hair to the spoon then gather a piece of material round the 'neck' and stick it in place. Pass the spoon handle through the neck, then stick the bottom of the skirt to the open end of the bottle. Cover the join with tape and a pretty ribbon. Add pipe-cleaner arms if you like.

GAMES A SOCIAL BABY CAN PLAY ALONE

Now that the baby is getting even more adventurous and better at picking things up, you will have to be very careful about what you let him play with on his own. Never leave him entirely alone, but if you have a playpen you can start to put him in it or in his cot for short periods of time to give yourself a break.

Your baby's desire to explore far outstrips his knowledge of what is good for him and his practice of running his tongue around objects could extend to those which could kill him. Even before he can crawl, he can move around by squirming and rolling. Make sure everything near him is safe for him to play with or to put into his mouth, and always keep within earshot. All houses with babies in them need to be 'babyproofed' and all babies need to be supervised.

First toys should move easily when touched, so hang them from a short length of ribbon or elastic and make sure they are in the way of waving arms and kicking legs. At first the baby may hit the toy by chance, but he will soon learn to do it on purpose.

Learning he can make things happen is an important step in any child's development. Encourage him by letting him hit things, by making a noise with a rattle and by coming when he calls you. Soon he will want to grab the toys, so make sure they are securely fixed. At first, as he reaches, he will have difficulty ignoring his hand – he reaches for the rattle but watches his hand instead. Slowly and cleverly he will begin to work out how to make the hand reach its goal.

Remember that babies move their hands, not the toys, to their mouths, so be careful that the handle of a wooden spoon does not get pushed down their throat or poke an eye as they bring it towards them.

Feeling and Exploring

Babies have to explore if they are to understand the relationship between how things look, feel and sound. At first their hands are not as skilful as their tongue and lips. The fact that the tongue magnifies everything it feels is an added bonus. Once they can move their fingers independently – at about nine months – they will begin to use their hands more.

KEEPING THINGS IN REACH   ●   In the first six months babies do not look for things they drop, they just grab those things that they can see. Offer a toy to your baby and he will drop whatever he is holding while he reaches for the new toy. To help keep toys within reach, tie them securely to one of the following:

An oven rack
A washing-up rack
A 'non-slip' bath mat
A sink mat.

Make sure there are no sharp edges, then fix the whole kit to the cot, high chair or playpen bars.

When he starts to be able to hold things, you can also leave a few loose toys near him, but make sure nothing is small enough to fit into his mouth. Later, when he starts to reach out for toys and to hold them in his hands, you can give him more things to play with on his own, but always check he cannot be harmed in any way.

FEELY • Once he can sit up on his own, you may find that he will enjoy a tabard or overall with lots of toys attached – a sort of wearable activity centre. Make sure that there are no sharp edges and that everything is securely fastened.

SOMETHING TO KICK ABOUT • Every now and then it is lovely to put the baby on a rug on the floor for a good nappy-free kick. Make sure it is warm enough, and put him where he can watch something interesting, such as curtains blowing in the wind or a mobile.

A BIT OF BLANKET • New-born babies do not miss us when we leave them, because, unless they see us, they forget we exist. This starts to change as they grow older, and at some time during the first year almost all babies become 'clingy'. I found at this stage that I felt rather smug to be the wanted object, but that it also made life much more demanding. Because they are beginning to know what it is like to miss somebody, babies at this time often latch on to comforters of some kind, from a piece of blanket to a thumb or a dummy. Research has firmly established that comfort objects are a good thing – a child who has learned to 'psych himself up' with a quick cuddle of a beloved teddy has learned how to cope with life! I do recommend that you try to get hold of an identical object before too long as, apart from a thumb, the comforter is almost bound to be lost at a later stage. It can be quite galling to hold up a well-deserved evening out just to search the house for a small square of blue blanket.

MOBILE
BABY

INTRODUCTION

There comes a moment – and it happens at different ages with different children – when your baby seems to take a sudden leap and become a small child. It is partly the physical changes that are noticeable, of course, and they can certainly be dramatic: your containable little bundle that could be propped up by cushions and guaranteed to stay put has become an increasingly mobile weapon of destruction. Whoever first described slow-moving traffic as 'crawling' could never have seen the speed-crawl of a determined baby. Nothing can now be considered safely out of his reach unless it is at adult-height and on a non-shakeable surface.

But the changes are more than physical. Although the baby may not be able to speak yet, he is beginning to understand. Showing him how to play with his toys will help him at this stage, because now he is ready to copy what you do. You realize one day that he is no longer just chewing and banging his toys – he is treating them differently. He puts the toy cup to his lips, he cuddles his teddy, he 'brrmms' his car. You get the feeling he is starting to remember the games you play together: something he enjoyed on Tuesday he will be ready for on Friday when you sit down in the same chair.

He plans. He seems to know what he wants in advance. He crawls across the room purposefully to fetch a car (or the Ming vase if you are less lucky) and then sits and plays with it, rather than playing with the car as he happens to come across it in his travels. Because he can plan, he can carry out more complex actions, and the toys and games for this period should reflect his growing skill.

The months between babyhood and the 'terrible twos' form one of the 'easy' stages that occur throughout our children's lives. It coincides with the achievement of much that the child has been working towards: it is not a time of great leaps and bounds of achievement, but of polishing and developing skills. He is more independent, so, although you have to watch him, you may be able to relax between demands, and at the end of the day he may be tired enough to snuggle down at seven and sleep through till morning. He can move, so he is no longer frustrated by things that are out of his reach, and he can communicate with you. In these months his capacity to remember and anticipate, plan and string actions together becomes obvious.

GAMES TO PLAY WITH A MOBILE BABY

Special Events

It is always easier to remember things if they are associated with exciting and unusual events. To a child, the daily routine gives a sense of security, but special outings are little islands of experience he will remember later. Remind him of them with books, stories and toys. For example, show him a picture of a bus the day after you visit a garage or look at a book about puppies after you visit the pet shop.

WHAT SHALL WE DO TODAY? ●

Look up your local bus garage in the phone book. These usually have wide open doors, so you don't need to go inside. The sheer volume of buses is the exciting part. If your child usually travels by car, then a bus ride would make an even better treat

Visit tractors, or cranes, or combine harvesters, or big diggers. Big, noisy machines were a favourite of my second child, and when they dug up the road a few doors down from us, I spent much of every morning standing outside the house holding him in my arms while he stared in endless fascination at the JCBs

Visit the pet shop. Obviously the more animals they have on display the better, but even the odd fish is interesting

Post a letter. This can be very popular. Let him carry the letter himself and lift him up so he can put it in the box. You may find that he will then want it back, which can be quite tricky

Buy bananas – or biscuits, or a cake for tea. Can he hold the money in a purse and carry the bananas home?

Hunt for cats. Wildlife is difficult for very small children to see – it tends, sensibly, to steer well clear of those dauntingly loving, sticky fingers – but cats and dogs and the occasional pigeon, duck or squirrel stay around long enough for him to point and shout at

Smell the flowers. He may not quite understand *how* to smell (often blowing down his nose), but it is fun trying

Watch the trains, or, if you are lucky enough, the boats

Walk (or push the buggy) through fallen leaves

Visit other babies at the clinic, a mother and baby group, the supermarket or a school as the children leave for home.

Or why not stay at home and:

**Have a picnic on a rug in the sitting room – or in the garden if you
have one**

Watch the clothes in the washing machine

Collect the letters

Carry the potatoes (possibly one by one!) to the sink

Sit in the empty box after you have unpacked the shopping

**Sit with a big bowl of rice, or cracked wheat or playdough, and let him
squeeze it through his hands.** Mashed potato is great fun too, if you can
bear the mess

Draw little faces on your fingers. He may be too young to enjoy having
puppets on his fingers, but he will like watching them on yours. He will
also enjoy putting play people into cars and planes

Eat sandwiches with faces on them – add features from bits of tomato,
cucumber and so on, or just draw a face with edible colouring on to the
bread or toast.

Cause and Effect

Your child has known for some time that he can make things happen. Now he knows before he does something what the end result will be. This is why toys with 'surprises', such as Jack-in-the-boxes, books and spinning tops delight. It is the anticipation of what is about to happen that is such fun.

Exploring takes on a new meaning at this stage. Now it is about seeing what will happen if. Give him boxes and bags with things hidden inside, paint to spread out, paper to scrunch up and throw, and anything he can shake, squeeze or spread.

HIS OWN DRAWER • There is nothing as exciting to a child as emptying the cupboard, drawer or bookcase – and few things more frustrating for parents than the endless replacing of things. Set aside one safe shelf or drawer just for him, and fill it with noisy keys, sheets of paper, old tennis balls and so on. Wedge the other drawers so he cannot open them. This also works very well with an old handbag, and may prevent him from emptying your real one – although babies seem to have an uncanny instinct for homing in on the things you would really rather they *didn't* reorganize for you.

LUCKY DIP • Fill a bucket, bag or carton with scrunched-up paper (or straw or polystyrene packaging if you are sure that he is past the 'into the mouth' stage). Hide a few little toys inside and let him find them. They needn't be new toys – finding a good old favourite can be just as much fun.

MESSY PAINT • He is too young for figurative work, but, boy, does he do great abstracts!

Put down a large groundsheet. Take some thick paint (see page 85). Pour it on to a low washable table or the tray of his high chair. Let him spread the paint with his hands. If you would like to hang on to the masterpiece for posterity you can take a print (see page 85).

This artistic exercise is best performed before bathtime – or out of doors where you have the garden hose handy!

PAINT SANDWICH   •   Spread a piece of cling film on the table. Mix a little powder paint with some paste to thicken it and put it on the cling film in blobs. Carefully place another piece of cling film over the top and seal the edges. Show him how to press the paint and move it about (more abstract art!).

SWISHING JARS   •

Half-fill a plastic jar with water and float a few corks or bits of wood in it. Screw on the lid. Tape it up for good measure.

Or, half-fill the jar with coloured water, add a spoonful or two of cooking oil, screw on the lid and tape it. Swish!

PAPER   •

Play tug-of-war with a box full of tissues
Roll up a ball of paper and throw it
Kick a ball of paper around the room

Wet some newspapers and squeeze

Post old empty envelopes and junk mail in the bin (Warning: this game can be dangerous. Nightly bin-checks may be needed to retrieve important letters and cheques).

Put lots of torn-up newspaper on the floor and sit with the baby in the middle. Throw the paper up into the air to make a snowstorm.

SLITHER   •

Take a box – a longish chocolate box would do – put something inside and tape down the lid. He will enjoy listening to the sounds the object makes as he moves the box this way and that.

GAMES A MOBILE BABY CAN PLAY ALONE

Starting to Build and Puzzle

There are many games which begin now and progress through childhood. Between years one and two children begin to build and stack, but not very skilfully. Give your child a few large bricks, particularly soft play bricks; it is worth buying the best you can afford (or choose a set you can add to later), as he will be playing with them for years. Saucepans or plastic cups can also be used for stacking.

Very simple two- or three-piece jigsaws are mastered in the second year. Small children find tray puzzles with little knobs to grasp easiest to handle. In choosing puzzles, bear in mind that the best ones for younger children show a picture on each piece.

Transport

We often think of puzzles and bricks as 'educational' toys. In fact, what they help to develop is a sense of achievement, planning and spatial abilities. But bikes and push-alongs do this too; on a larger scale the problems are much the same.

Once he is mobile, he will love a sit-and-ride, a toddler truck or even a small trike. My children played and played with these, and one of my sons went one way round and round the kitchen table so fast and for such lengths of time that we used to wonder if he would grow up with one leg shorter than the other. Some of these vehicles can be extremely noisy. Make sure that you can live with – or switch off! – the sound effects.

A useful trick is to hide toys in bags or in the secret place in the back of his truck – it will keep him happy for hours.

Pretending

SOMETHING HE CAN USE TO BE LIKE YOU • A mobile baby loves to copy. Find him a few saucepans, a teaset, a toy drill or a hammer. Later he might like a broom or toy vacuum cleaner, a duster or a washing-up bowl. Cleaning has a fascination at this age that unfortunately doesn't seem to last – it is hard to remember now that my nineteen-year-old daughter once enjoyed washing tables more than anything else.

FRIENDS • As your child enters his second year, all the soft toys he has been accumulating begin to find new life. Now a teddy may ride on his truck with him, and in a year or two his toys will all take bit parts in endless pretend games. If you draw these toys into the games you share, he will slowly begin to play more with them on his own.

TODDLER

INTRODUCTION

This is the age that at the same time can be the most enchanting and the most frustrating of all. A pair of chubby arms thrown round your neck and a messy kiss bring a glow to your heart, but the endless demands, the tantrums and the grizzling can dim that glow pretty sharpish.

It is enchanting how ready he is to share everything with you. Probably nobody will ever love and admire you as uncritically or with the whole-hearted joy and need of your happy toddler. Not a cat or bus passes without him showing it to you and, as his language improves, he provides a running commentary on your day, making you look at things around you through his eyes. Soon he is taking every opportunity to engage you in conversation, and the favourite opening gambit is WHY? It can drive you to distraction, but, as you are his main source of information and as the world is such an extraordinary and surprising place, you really cannot blame him for asking questions constantly. There are times, however, when it can be hard to take:

Parent: **Let's have lunch now.**
Child: **Why?**
Parent: **Because you must be hungry.**
Child: **Why?**
Parent: **Well, you haven't eaten anything since breakfast.**
Child: **Why?**
Parent (slightly losing loving, patient tone): **Because we were out shopping this morning and you didn't have your elevenses.**
Child: **Why?**
Parent (altogether losing loving, patient tone): **It's difficult to find milk and biscuits in the ironmonger's.**
Child: **Why?**
Parent (gritting teeth): **Because they don't sell that kind of thing.**
Child: **Why?**
Parent (in raised tone of voice): **Biscuit crumbs might get mixed up with the nails and hammers.**
Child: **Why?**

Parent (tense and speaking rather wildly): **They don't have room to keep them separate.**
Child: **Why?**
Parent (unnecessarily loudly): **Because the shop isn't big enough.**
Child: **Why?**
Parent (shouting): **Rents in this area are particularly high and since the onset of the recession few shops can afford to expand their businesses and, indeed, many of them are having a hard time surviving as it is. I don't think, in any case, that when that nice Mr Smith opened his ironmonger's, he ever had any intention or desire to sell milk and biscuits but presumed he would stick to the more traditional ironmongery goods such as saucepans, kettles, bin-liners and so on.**
PAUSE
Child: **Why?**
Parent (completely losing cool): **BECAUSE I SAY SO!**

(Now didn't you promise yourself you'd *never* say that to *your* child?)

Physically, too, he is questioning everything by poking, prodding, fiddling and fidgeting. What happens if I squeeze, or poke, or roll it flat? Does it make a noise if I drop it? Does it stick? Can I make it into another shape?

These are the easy questions. There are harder ones to take: What happens if I say no? What happens if I disobey or throw my dinner on the floor?

Most playing will still be done with you, but at this stage you will begin to find activities that can engage the attention for longer spans of solitary playing – still, of course, within your sight, because, however apparently safe the game, a toddler can find the most inventive ways of hurting himself.

> Suddenly he is not a baby any more. He is less impulsive, more cautious, at the same time more easy to manage and much, much more difficult. You can take your eyes off him occasionally, communicate more easily and let him feed and amuse himself. However, now there is another difference: he exerts his will, he says no! It is a step forward, a move towards independence and a shaping of an individual personality, but for parents used to a child who did their bidding unquestioningly it can be difficult.

Combined with this desire to exert his will is a jumble of other emotions. The terrible twos are basically a battle between two people: you and your child. You need to negotiate his freedoms and yours, his dependency and yours, the times when you must be obeyed and when he can have his say. As in all things, social skills lay the foundation for wider learning. The underlying message is that there are rules about how people act and most other things too. He tests these out as he plays with sand and water, paint, cars and construction kits.

Imitation and Pretending

Children under four do not construct pretend worlds for themselves: they imitate the worlds we teach them to construct. This may seem a minor point, but it has major implications. If nobody shows a toddler how to play pretend games, he will not pretend. Such games involve imitation, memory, planning, social skills, communication and interaction; they also incorporate fine motor movements and co-ordination – in fact, most things we want our toddlers to learn.

SIMON SAYS   ●   The child must copy all the actions:

Simon says touch your nose
You touch your nose and let him copy you
Simon says stand on one leg
Simon says jump up
Simon says clap your hands.

When he gets older you can add the sophisticated variation that he must only do *what Simon says* so that if you suddenly say 'Touch your nose', he mustn't do it.

At this age you can both have great fun with songs that have actions to them. This is one of my favourites that I remember from my childhood:

I'm a little teapot
Short and stout.
Here is my handle.
Bend one arm and put your hand on your waist

Here is my spout.
Stick out the other arm
When I get all steamed up,
Hear me shout.
Tip me over
Bend over sideways
And pour me out!
Keep bending!

And there is always:

Head and shoulders, knees and toes, knees and toes,
Head and shoulders, knees and toes, knees and toes,
And eyes and ears, and a mouth and a nose,
Head and shoulders, knees and toes, knees and toes.

The obvious pointing actions go with this verse. Older children enjoy missing out the first word and performing the action silently:

... and shoulders, knees and toes, knees and toes,
... and shoulders, knees and toes, etc.

In the next verses the child loses shoulders, then knees and so on, but still goes through the required motions.

Also try:

One, two, three, four, five,
Once I caught a fish alive,
Six, seven, eight, nine, ten,
Then I let it go again.

Why did I let it go?
Because it bit my finger so.
Which finger did it bite?
This little finger on the right.

Or:

The wheels on the bus go round and round (with its wonderfully politically incorrect verse 'The mums on the bus go chatter, chatter, chatter')
My bonny lies over the ocean
Down by the station
Here is the church, and here is the steeple.

WAKE UP •   This is the age for bringing his soft toys to life. Act out simple stories – trips to the shop, riding in the car. Walk the teddies through their paces.

Reading

Like speaking, the aptitude for learning the shapes of letters and grasping the concepts that they mean something when joined together into words and that those words are written from left to right comes at very different ages for different children. Sitting together and looking at picture books with words printed underneath and reading them out loud helps enormously to encourage this ability. And, of course, reading stories to your child is one of life's greatest pleasures: sit him on your lap, open a good book with plenty of pictures and off you go. You will soon find out which is the favourite, and then you may well be reading that particular story over and over and over again…several times a day for several months…until you feel certain that if that hungry caterpillar eats its way through one more nice green leaf you may well have a nervous breakdown.

It is fun, too, to make up stories, particularly at bedtime, but the snag is that when a repeat performance is requested you will probably have forgotten much of the previous night's brilliant improvisation. He won't have, and woe betide you if your tale isn't exactly the same in every detail.

The earliest books should contain pictures of objects: shoes, cats, cups and animals. The best ones are clearly drawn and brightly coloured, but they don't have to be realistic. At first he will be too busy turning the pages to wait for you to read the words, but as he gets older he will begin to understand enough language to listen to the story as long as there is not much more than one line of text per page. Favourites are firmly rooted in everyday life: hungry animals, naughty babies, walks to the shops. By about the age of three he will want a little more storyline; by four, something altogether more fantastic.

One of the great innovations over the last few years has been the introduction of books with little flaps or finger holes. Many of these are very successful with toddlers.

> Cuddling up to read a book together first and foremost promotes a feeling of love and security. It also involves following a storyline and predicting what comes next, and it helps enlarge the child's vocabulary and teaches him how to construct more complex sentences. In addition, your child will learn to distinguish the little sounds that make up words by listening to rhymes and rhythms as you read to him – another skill that is vital when he starts to read on his own.

CATALOGUES AND ALBUMS • Children's clothes and toy catalogues have all the elements of an enjoyable book: brightly coloured pictures of lots of familiar things. Photograph albums are also firm favourites; he may not recognize himself in the pictures, but he will know you, and as he grows older he will become increasingly interested in himself as a baby.

NURSERY RHYMES • I remember being told when I had my first baby that singing to her would help her learn to read. This seemed mysterious and I couldn't quite see the connection, but I suppose it is all to do with rhythm and meaning. I certainly did sing to her a great deal – mostly from a surprising instinct to do so – and she did learn to read relatively easily, but I cannot claim any scientific proof that the two things were linked.

Nursery rhymes, counting songs, action rhymes and lullabies are all a delightful part of our culture, and generations of parents have discovered how they soothe and teach children. Don't ignore the old favourites – they have become so for the good reason that countless children over the years must have said 'Again!'.

The next few games involve a gentle progression to help your child to listen, pretend and tell stories:

HOW BIG ARE YOU?★ ● A child's earliest language is sign language. Encourage his understanding of words with simple word games:

> *How big are you?*
> **Stretch your arms right up high**
> *How small are you?*
> **Get down low**
> *How quiet are you?*
> **Touch your fingers to your lips**
>
> **Have him copy what you do.**

WHAT DO WE DO?★ ●

> *When we see a picture of a cake?*
> **Eat it**
> *A picture of a rabbit?*
> **Stroke it gently**
> *A picture of a teddy?*
> **Cuddle it.**

WHAT DOES IT SAY?★ ● A picture book of animals is all that is needed for this game:

> *What does the cat say?*
> *What does the cow say?*

★ These games are also good for older children with language difficulties. Children with special needs often find themselves isolated from children of their own age, because a two-year-old, for instance, is only just learning how to play himself and cannot give the extra encouragement or consideration special children need. However, parents can play these games with children on a one-to-one basis.

LEARNING WHAT LITTLE WORDS MEAN •

Put the cow *on top of* the house
Put the car *inside* the barn
Put the pig *under* the bed
Put Mummy's money back *into* her purse.

This last one is worth practising – it continues to be useful right through to the teen years and beyond.

Making Plans★

The plans children make are simple at first. Starting with the 'I'll crawl over there and empty the drawer' kind of planning, they soon adopt more ambitious and complicated ideas: 'I'll open that cupboard so I can get the flour out'; 'I'll fill my plastic teapot with water so I can empty it over the side of the bath'. By about two and a half a child might even take himself off to the park if someone leaves the gate open, so be vigilant.

> To plan you need to be able to retain a number of things in your mind at the same time. Small children find plans difficult because they only hold two or three things at a time in their minds, not five to nine the way adults do. This means that not only do they have difficulty with long and complex sentences, but they also do not always perceive the consequences of their actions. Helping them to plan is really helping them to learn tricks to overcome these limitations.

FIND THE OTHER ONE • Children have remarkable visual memories. Although they don't search systematically, they can often remember exactly where something is (we exploit this talent in my nine-year-old when one of us has lost something).

This game is best played with pairs of plastic animals (perhaps from a Noah's Ark set) or something similar. Put one of each pair in reasonably obvious places around the house. Put the others in a bag, then pull out one at a time, saying: 'Here's one, where is the other one?' Once your child understands this game, you will be surprised how well he can play it.

★Children with learning difficulties need a great deal of encouragement to plan ahead. Break tasks down into stages and concentrate on one stage at a time.

HOUSEWORK • Yes, I'm sorry to say that this is the time when you have to start accepting help with the housework. Dusting is quite a good task to begin with, as long as you restrict it to safe, solid objects – don't let him loose with a J-cloth on the Staffordshire china just yet. Washing up can be enjoyable, but don't choose this particular chore if you are in a hurry to get things done; the amount of setting up beforehand (a safe chair to stand on, warm water, unbreakable objects to wash, etc.) and clearing up of sloshed soapy water afterwards can make you very frazzled.

THE ORDER OF THINGS • Planning is emphasized when order is needed, or rules have to be followed. Look out for jigsaws in which a line of cars is arranged so that they go from small at one end to big at the other. Russian dolls that fit inside each other are good too. Relate size to something he can understand; for example, big might go with Mummy, medium with the toddler and small with the baby. Don't have too many in-betweens; three sizes is quite enough at first.

Getting Physical

From wobbly walks around the furniture to running, climbing and pushing a toy wheelbarrow, the physical changes now can be fast and dramatic. The toy shops are full of toys to see a small child through this stage. Baby walkers can be useful in moderation, but never use them anywhere near the top of the stairs or large windows, patio doors, etc. As soon as a child is steady on his feet, he will enjoy playing with a push-along toy on a stick. Because he won't try to pull himself up with one of these, they are quite safe even for the unsteady. Other larger push-alongs should be avoided until he has spent at least a month walking without support.

Once he is ready to ride, there is a large and exciting choice of suitable toys. It is particularly worth investing in a sturdy, well-made sit-and-ride, as it will undergo extensive and ferocious road testing. But do remember to test the horn, hooter or bell to determine if you will be able to bear hearing it more or less continuously over the next few years.

Practice makes perfect. Nowhere is this more true than when we talk of physical skills. Whether catching, throwing, balancing or moving through space, there is only one way to learn how to co-ordinate movement of the hand and eye and that is to practise.

A PLAYGROUND AT HOME • Hiding and finding is one of *the* great toddler games. Sometimes you might like to make it extra fun by pulling out the sofa just far enough for him to be able to crawl in at one end and out at the other. First chase him from behind and run around and meet him face on. Then you crawl through and let him do the finding. Or:

Make a safe obstacle course
Crawl through a box tunnel (open at both ends)
Pass a hoop over his head
Have him push a soft ball with his nose
Stand on a low chair
Walk backwards.

A PLAYGROUND OUTSIDE •

On a windy day let the wind almost blow you over
On a wet day get under a big umbrella
On a sunny day get out the garden hose
On a snowy day – just get out there!

BALL GAMES★ •   Until your child can aim, he needs something soft enough to throw but not cause damage. Foam balls are ideal – large ones to catch and kick, small ones to roll and throw.

Rolling the ball: He sits with his legs open and you roll the ball to him

Goal-keeper: Use the door frame; roll the ball and let him kick it away from the goal

Throwing: You will find yourself lungeing all over the place in desperate attempts to catch his throws at first, but gradually they will become aimed more in your general direction.

★ These games are good for older children who need support to stand. You could use two strong chairs as the goal posts.

MAKING A BEAN BAG • You can make bean bags very easily. You can use any shape you like, but a rectangle is easiest to throw and catch. Cut out two pieces of strong colourful material, about 15 x 10 centimetres (6 x 4 inches). Sew them together firmly, leaving a hole big enough to fill with rice, dried peas or haricot beans (don't use kidney beans, which are poisonous when raw). Sew up the hole securely. For a washable version, use very strong material and fill the rectangle with fish grit from a pet shop.

An extra-large bag can be filled with plastic egg boxes. It makes a lovely noise and doesn't hurt if someone gets in the path of an inexpert throw.

GAMES A TODDLER CAN PLAY ALONE

Imitation and Pretending

A BOX TO SIT IN★   •   You will need:

One big cardboard box from the supermarket check-out, with or without a cushion inside
One child to sit in the box

It may not seem much of a game, but toddlers love it. Later you could fix on pretend wheels, a roof or windows. For the moment, he will be quite happy to have it just as it comes.

A HOUSE UNDER THE TABLE   •   You will need a small blanket or sheet and a washing line, a clothes horse or a table. Throw the blanket over the support and you have instant magic. Young children and animals have

★ If the box is wedged with cushions, an unsteady child will enjoy sitting in it too. It sometimes helps if you can wedge his bottom into a pot!

a fascination for small spaces. You can put in his teaset and a few teddies, but at first he will be happy just to sit. All my children loved creating these secret places, and as they grew older the constructions became more complicated. Corners of blankets were tucked into drawers to keep them up, cushions were bulldog-clipped by their fringes to make doors and sheets were stretched precariously between armchairs.

MR POSTMAN • Or Father Christmas, if the time is right (or even if it is midsummer!). All you need is a pillowcase or a small bag and something to deliver.

A HAT TO START THE DRESSING-UP BOX • Dressing-up in earnest starts at about two and a half, but before that pulling hats on can give huge pleasure. He may not know how to play at being a bus driver or a policeman, but he will enjoy sitting around in the hat none the less.

TOOLS FOR HIS TRADE • Early imitation and pretend games centre around household activities. Toddlers enjoy:

Teasets
Saucepans
Tools
Vacuum cleaners
Bags

And, if there is a new baby in the house, don't forget the dolls and pushchairs.

A MECHANICS BOARD★ • This is an activity centre for an older child. You will need a large piece of wooden shelving about 90 × 60

★ This makes a good activity centre for an older child with special needs.

centimetres (3 × 2 feet). Smooth out any rough edges and varnish it, then add some of the following:

A door knob and a door handle
A bolt and a lock
An old wall-mounted telephone
A mirror tile
A light switch
A button and buttonhole cut from an old coat
A zip
A strip of Velcro
A plastic hook and something to hang on it
A short piece of curtain rod with wooden rings.

Fix the whole thing to the wall at child height.

Quiet Time

Consolidation is the sort of complex word small children like to say. When psychologists talk about consolidation they mean that information is brought together and laid down as a relatively permanent form of knowledge. You might call it cogitating – standing back and seeing the connections between things. Children spend so much of their day finding out about the world that they really need their quiet times to get it all into perspective. At intervals throughout the day they must also relieve stresses and generally recharge their batteries.

READING • There is something immensely satisfying about seeing a child curled up with a good book, and something that makes us feel guilty about a child sitting in front of a television or computer game. I think it is important to see both in perspective – Caxton was probably accused of disrupting family life and preventing children from getting fresh air and exercise when he first made the written word available to the public. There is no doubt that reading provides knowledge (and great pleasure) and stimulates the imagination, but there is no need to panic if a child doesn't seem to take to it naturally. The more you insist on a child reading, the more he will rebel against it. Read *with* him (see page 97) as often as you can, and sit and read by yourself occasionally. Remember that children learn mostly by example. Provide plenty of interesting, colourful books and comics in a place where he can easily find them, and at some point he will probably pick one up on his own and take an interest.

TV AND VIDEOS • It is, of course, very tempting to sit a young child in front of the television just to get a few minutes' peace – and all of us do it. So we should! I don't think there is any need to feel that television is never a good thing – as a stimulator and entertainer for children it can hardly be bettered if it is used in moderation. Try to choose programmes that you think your child will particularly enjoy, rather than turn the TV on at any time. Teach him that there is an off switch and use it at the end of each programme; don't leave it on until there is something else to do.

Toddlers use TV to soothe rather than to learn. Like an adult, a young child needs floppy times when he does nothing – time to cuddle up, suck his thumb, hold tight to his mug and twiddle his hair. For many children

TV acts like a signal which heralds the resting time that comes between bursts of learning.

How much TV and video should he watch each day? Five hours is always too much. More than one hour at a stretch is probably too much unless he is cuddled up with you.

Making Plans

It is always a good idea to ask your child for help; it makes him feel important and useful, and one day it actually *will* be helpful. In the right mood 'Could you dust the table for me please?' brings a beam of pleasure and a five-minute stretch of happy solo activity. A feather duster on a stick is very popular.

WATERING THE GARDEN   •   You need:

A little watering can
A plant in need of water

As a special treat you can let him use the garden hose, but supervise him, or the plants – and his clothes – will get overwatered.

PICKING UP TOYS ● Of course you could do it faster without your child's help, but it is a very good habit to try to instil, and at this age it is still fun.

TOYS TO ENCOURAGE PLANS ●

Simple jigsaws
Play people that slot into buses
Toys with handles that turn to make something happen
Shape sorters with extra surprises
Simple construction kits like Duplo or Sticklebricks bricks.

Getting Physical

LETTING OFF STEAM★ ● Children have a natural safety valve: glee and wild excitable rough and tumble play. You can stop children racing around for a while, but it is only a delaying tactic. Confine them in the car and you can feel the temperature rising and the pent-up energy mounting until you open the door and they burst out like popcorn. Children often egg each other on to wilder and wilder games, whereas a solitary child might need to be encouraged to let off steam.

INSTANT EXCITEMENT ● Put some pillows or a couple of duvets on the floor and let him jump off the stairs. Be careful – he may have more courage than sense and you must monitor the number of steps from which it is safe to jump. Small children should jump on to the floor and then fall on to the cushions; older children can dive directly on to the soft landing place.

MAKING A GRAND-PRIX COURSE ● This game requires a sit-and-ride – ideally one that is easily manoeuvrable. If it is not, then try crawling instead. It is great fun for the child to go back to crawling once he has learned to walk. Make a safe and simple course around the sofa, down a ramp, into the hall and through a tunnel made by lifting curtains over the table.

★ This sort of play is especially difficult for children with physical disabilities or children with learning problems who might have trouble initiating their own 'glee'. Water, which supports movement, gives them more freedom. Tickling, swinging, dancing, pushing their chairs fast or shouting under a bridge are all good ways of releasing energy. You could also try sitting them on the washing machine and letting them feel the vibrations as a way of helping them to relax.

THROWING NEWSPAPER BALLS   •

You will need old newspaper and two players
Roll up balls of newspaper and throw them at each other

For a slightly more sophisticated version, make a 'fence' with pillows and throw the balls over it (good Wimbledon training this bit).

WALKING THE DOG
AND OTHER FRIENDS★   •

Ducks, dogs, cars, telephones –
almost anything can be taken
for a walk around the house.

★ Moving snakes and other toys are
interesting for children who can only watch.

You can also make something yourself. These friendly snakes are very popular:

An old double-layer woollen scarf with a sock stuffed into one end and tied in place

A few cotton reels on a string clatter nicely. Loop the string around the end reel

Six lavatory paper cardboard tubes painted bright green. Put eyes and red fangs on one, then thread them on to the string. Use tape to secure the string to the last roll, then stuff an old sock into the first roll to keep the string in place.

Remember never to leave a small child alone with enough string to wrap around his neck. Make the lead short and don't be tempted to put a bobble on the end – bobbles can be swallowed.

OVER AND OVER • If you can find a grassy bank, why not roll down it? Better still, make it a special outing. The younger children may need you to roll them over, but as they get older they will need no encouragement. We all loved this as children, and I still get a twinge of excitement when I see a good smooth grassy hill, but then I remember I'm a sensible grown-up person with aching bones and fast-disappearing brain cells, and I stop myself just in time.

CLIMBING • A two-year-old often has more courage than sense, and climbing frames for this age should not be very high. Even when he is much older, you may still find him holding on for dear life. Light plastic tubular frames that can be taken apart and rebuilt in different shapes are ideal if you have space for them. They are particularly good on the lawn because you can lift them up to mow the grass. If you don't have the money or space for a climbing frame, try:

Bunk beds
Walking on low walls – hold his hand
Climbing up a five-bar gate
Finding a suitable log or tree

A line of upturned paint pots filled with sand and with the lids firmly hammered on
A playground

An old armchair is a good soft climbing surface, but it is a good idea to ban climbing on any furniture that you care about (and always insist on shoes off for indoor mountaineering).

Playing with the Elements

It is often said that when children play with the elements they are acting like scientists finding out the rules that govern the world. Although the scientific rules small children come up with are invariably wrong, and their mathematical principles faulty, they do learn a great deal about cause and effect and testing hypotheses.

WATER • There is enormous fascination with water at this age. Even if you have nowhere outside that the child can play, it doesn't mean he has to go without water play. If you spread a plastic sheet or tablecloth on the

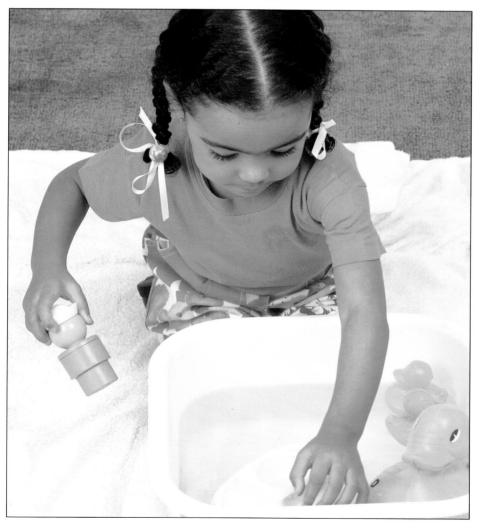

floor and put a small basin of water out with a selection of toys, spoons, plastic beakers and so on, he may splash about happily for some time. Always make sure that he is within view, of course, as toddlers can drown in tiny amounts of water.

AT THE SINK   •   There are two different ways a child can play at the sink: with a stream or with a bowl of water (again, always within your sight).

With a stream he can:
Fill a cup
Listen to the sound it makes on a cake tin
Watch how lukewarm water makes a hole in ice cubes
Fill a toy teapot and pour it out
Watch how a patch of wetness spreads through a dry cloth
Wash his hands.

With a bowl of water he can:

Wet a cloth and wring it
Wet a sponge and let it drip
Wet a piece of plastic and watch the water on its surface
Sink a cup
Float a wooden peg
Watch how an oil slick makes patterns on the surface of the water
(very good training for future environmental awareness!).

In the garden he can:

Water the plants
Make wet footprints on the paved parts
Paint the wall with a pot of water and a paintbrush
Run in and out of the garden sprinkler
Make patterns with a squeezy bottle full of water
Stamp in the puddles.

PLAYING WITH SAND   •   There are two sorts of sand: wet and dry. Dry flows, wet sticks. Dry sand is played with like water; wet sand is more like playdough. It is fun to explore both, but at the youngest age he will probably find dry sand more interesting.

CARE OF SANDPITS • Garden sandpits are a delight not only to children but also to cats. It is dangerous and unhygienic to leave a sandpit uncovered, so always sweep the sand back into the pit and cover it safely when your child has finished playing in it.

Small children do not need a lot of playthings; they will often be quite happy just sitting in the sand and letting it run through their fingers, or pushing it about with their hands.

You don't have to use a serious, purpose-built pit. Try:

A small wooden box with a lid
A solid drawer from an old chest of drawers
A washing-up bowl
A small solid paddling pool
A tyre.

You can make a lid from a circle of cloth held in place with elastic or a tie. It doesn't need to be waterproof unless you have no drainage at the bottom, but it must be dog- and cat-proof. Always use soft sand: builders' sand is too sharp and will hurt his delicate skin.

INDOOR SAND • A child can play with sand indoors if you have a suitable container and a large groundsheet. He won't need much sand – a half-filled washing-up bowl is plenty. You can also use a bag of couscous, sugar or rice instead of sand. A colander, jug or funnel makes it more interesting.

Modelling and Painting

Carrots are always better inducements to progress than sticks, and here are some fine opportunities for offering your child some really juicy 'carrots'. One of his pictures on the wall says he can do something you value, which is very special when he is only two and rather too aware of his limitations. Helping your child gain confidence is worth a thousand other lessons.

MODELLING • Playdough is such a simple substance, but it can give hours of fun. It can be shaped, coloured, rolled and cut out, squidged and pulled. You can set up a pretend cookery table with harmless plastic tools, little dishes and toy frying pans and leave him to make endless plates of delicious 'food'. Plastic biscuit cutters are wonderful with playdough, and even if the odd piece does go in his mouth, it won't do any harm. The saltiness will prevent most children from eating too much.

HOME-MADE PLAYDOUGH •

8oz/250g flour
8oz/250g salt
2 tablespoons cooking oil
a little powder paint mixed with water
extra water to mix

Mix everything together, knead it gently, then warm the dough in a pan until you have a soft lump. Give it to the child to play with while it is still warm.

You can vary the proportions to make stiffer doughs for modelling and softer ones for rolling and squeezing. Put them in plastic bags and they will keep for a week or so at least in a cool place.

PAINTING★ • Start a small child off with short, fat non-toxic crayons which are easy to hold. Most toddlers enjoy messing in paint with their hands and fingers, and later they will be able to use a small domestic paint brush of about 1 centimetre ($\frac{1}{2}$ inch) or a stubby artist's brush. Mix powder

★ Children who are clumsy or have poor hand control will always find it easier to paint with their hands and feet. Card is better for them to use than paper because it does not rip, but it is not always available. For children with limited hand use, it is easiest to let them paint straight on to a washable surface and then take a print of their picture (see page 85).

paint with water into a creamy thickness – thin paint will soak into the paper too much.

Keep any scrap paper that comes your way if it has a clean side. It is lovely not to have to be stingy with drawing and painting paper – old wallpaper, wallpaper lining, computer print-outs, old paper bags, wrapping paper – beg and borrow as much as you can. I was able to give my children old scripts to paint on; many moving speeches have since been covered in portraits of teddies or of Mummy or Daddy.

At first he will simply move his hand up and down to make a rather shapeless mess. Later he will move his hand around, forming interlacing circles. Finally he will learn to take his crayon or brush off the paper and put it back on again. It is only after he has passed through all three stages that he will begin to draw recognizable shapes and patterns, and even then they may be recognizable only to him. Be ready to admire some inscrutable blobs of colour and try not to commit yourself too quickly: 'What a lovely tree!', you might say fondly of his picture of the postman.

HOME-MADE PAINT •

**1 dessertspoon cornflour or 2 dessertspoons plain flour
8fl oz/250ml water with food colouring or powder paint added**

Mix together and heat until it is the thickness of custard.

MAKING A PRINT •   Put a blob or two of paint on a washable table. Let the child mess it into a lovely picture, then take a print: put a piece of paper over the artwork and press it lightly, perhaps rolling it gently with a rolling pin. Lift it off, then repeat the process a couple of times – often the second or third print is the best.

FINGER PAINT •   Small children sometimes find it easier to paint with their fingers, hands or even their feet. Give them card for this, or the back of washable wallpaper – it is less likely to rip.

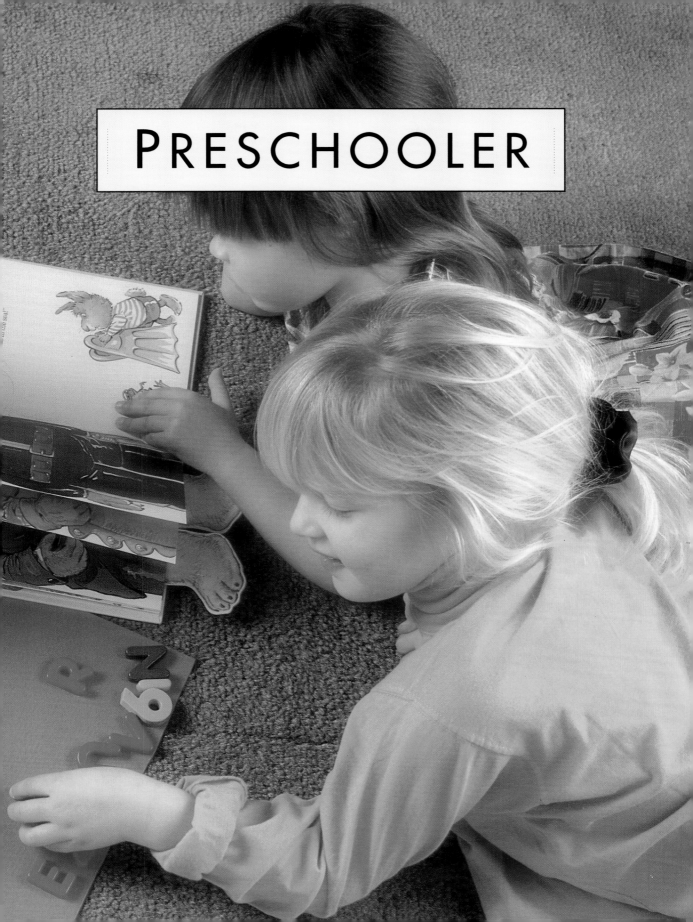

PRESCHOOLER

INTRODUCTION

One day you are sitting on the sofa and your child asks you if your headache is better. It hits you with a mixture of delight and sadness that he is not a baby any more. Although growing up is a gradual process, it often appears to happen in sudden bursts, physically as well as mentally. I swear my children stay roughly the same height for a few months, then, after a period of eating more than you would think possible for small human beings, they leap a couple of inches and their feet burst out of their shoes from one day to the next. From pointing at the cat and saying 'miaow', your baby is now asking you to explain the mysteries of life (I'm still working on that one).

Your child is better at expressing his fears and his feelings; his language may be simple, but he can gossip and tell you what he wants. He may even be starting to learn that persuasion can work better than lying on the floor and screaming. He learns by experiment, and by watching what others do and copying how they do it (and sometimes his attempts at being 'you' are far from flattering).

Although he is still boisterous and noisy, there are more quiet times, and in the right mood he will amuse himself with some toys or books while you make lunch or sit down for a few minutes with the paper and a cup of tea. He may have started playschool, where he will become more used to the company of other children, and will probably show a greater willingness to sit and 'work' at some writing, modelling or playing with Lego when he is at home. You could try to provide him with a little desk of his own to sit at. There are cheap plastic table and chair sets – for sale in places such as garages – which do very well and can be used inside or out in the garden.

Your preschooler is a charming mixture of baby and child. One minute he is very grown-up and independent; the next he is running back to you for a reassuring cuddle. As he becomes more and more a person in his own right, you should feel proud that the love and security that surrounds him is giving him the confidence to begin to break away.

I have not divided this section into games to play with your child or for him to play on his own, as by this stage it is very variable, and only you know under what conditions it is safe for him to be left alone to play. Don't forget that, however independent he is becoming, you must always be nearby – children can be extraordinarily inventive in the ways they hurt themselves.

Getting into the Rhythm⋆

Whether it is a spoon to bang on a saucepan, a real tambourine or just clapping hands to the music on the radio, the extraordinary communicatory powers of music can clearly be seen. The more you can encourage singing, dancing and an awareness of rhythm, the earlier your child is likely to become 'musical' and to develop a real love for it. It is far too early for most children to copy a complicated rhythm, but not too soon to try a simple one. Clap along to a pop song with a foot-tapping rhythm. Jog him on your knee in time to a bossa nova. Your dream of lying on the sofa listening to your little angel tripping lightly through a Mozart sonata on the piano may not come true for a few more years, but you may as well get off to a good start.

> In the early stages, learning about music is largely learning how to listen and how to make sounds. It is something that is easy for you and your child to do together, as music is naturally a social activity and a way of communicating. Your role is to reinforce what he learns, to help him to segregate the sounds and to introduce the shared emotional element which is so much a part of our enjoyment.

TRY THESE FOR SOUND   •

A biscuit tin hit with a wooden spoon
A saucepan or two hit with a wooden spoon
Two wooden bricks (or matchboxes) with a piece of sandpaper stuck to one side of each brick, which can be rubbed together†
Milk bottle tops in a stiff paper bag‡
Spoons to bang together.

⋆ A child with hearing loss can feel the vibration of your lips if you put them next to his skin and count 'one-a', 'two-a' as you dance with him in your arms.

† If your child has difficulty using both hands, stick one piece of sandpaper to the table.

‡ This makes a super large rattle for an older child.

MAKING A SET OF SHAKERS • Shakers are fun to make – older children will love helping – and can be used to accompany music on the radio or cassette and to dance to made-up songs. Don't expect a very young child to be rhythmical naturally – most children need lots of practice. Use all kinds of music – dance-bands, classical, rock, reggae, jazz, ballet, opera – anything and everything.

You will need: tubes, tins, small plastic jars, rice, dried peas or beans, bells, spaghetti, paper clips, PVA glue, insulating tape.

Cardboard tubes with metal bottoms and plastic tops make ideal shakers. Drinking chocolate, spices, sweets, stacking crisps and cheese biscuits all come in suitable containers of varying sizes.

Put a few dried peas in one tube, a little rice in another and some bits of spaghetti in a third. Smear PVA glue around the lid and stick it securely in place. After the glue has dried, you can strengthen the seal with insulating tape. Experiment with other containers: plastic shampoo bottles, metal tins and family-sized matchboxes. Try other fillings for different sounds: bells from the pet shop or haberdashery, paper clips, beads.

Ping-pong balls – or cat balls with bells inside – can be used to make giant shakers in a large biscuit tin sealed with tape.

MUSICAL INSTRUMENTS TO BUY★ ●

A cassette recorder. The child can listen and sing along to recorded music or mark the beat with a shaker; a cassette player is also wonderful for playing recorded stories. Look for one specially designed for small fingers
A tambourine
A drum
A referee's whistle (as long as you have tolerant neighbours)
A kazoo.

Don't invest in the Stradivarius just yet. When it comes to learning a 'proper' instrument, you should certainly start by hiring. If your child changes his mind about which instrument he is going to master as often as my children and I did, hiring is the only option.

★ Let children who have hearing difficulties feel the vibrations of a really good drum.

MUSIC WHILE YOU SHOUT • Some nursery schools in Japan set aside a special time each day when the children can make as much noise as they like. It is signalled by a particular record, and 'noise time' stops when the music stops. After five minutes of abandoned wildness, the children are ready to sit down quietly to lunch. This can be a useful technique just before bedtime, although you may have to allow five or ten minutes of calming-down time afterwards as a buffer — rather like the last few minutes of an exercise class. Also use it for those times when you know 'it will end in tears' (*wasn't* it annoying when your parents used to say that and they were *right*?) or when you feel a tantrum brewing. On days when you are on a shorter fuse than usual it may be worth joining in.

MUSIC WHILE YOU WORK • Since most things in a Japanese household are done on the floor, the end of the morning session at nursery school can look chaotic, with playdough, paints and sand everywhere. One nursery has an easy answer: the clean-up music, in their case a selection of Disney songs, including 'Hi ho, hi ho, it's off to work we go!'. Once the music is on so is the race to get everything picked up before the music ends. I've tried this recently at home with my teenage daughter in her bedroom but, unfortunately, it doesn't seem to have quite the same effect. The bribes that can be used to persuade small children to tidy up ('we'll have a lovely drink when we've finished', 'if you clear everything up we'll go to the playground') just don't seem to work past a certain age. At nineteen it would take a Nicole Fahri suit or a small Mercedes at minimum.

LISTEN •

> **Turn off the music – don't speak, put your fingers on your lips, sit very quiet and listen. . . What can you hear? The clock ticking, a car in the distance, a bird singing, the fridge humming. All the sounds of silence**
> **Listen on a snowy day**
> **Listen to the rain**
> **Listen in the middle of a busy street. Are there any birds?**

Getting into Step

At this age a child responds to music with his whole body. He hears, he feels, he moves. Moving to music comes naturally; it hardly needs your encouragement. He may not be a Nureyev, but his swaying and stomping will give him great pleasure and it is a good way to let off steam on a rainy day. My fractious two-year-old could always be soothed by watching my eight-year-old daughter practising her ballet. It reduced him to hysterical giggles; I'm still not quite sure why.

> Moving to music helps the child to listen to the notes and rhythm. To dance formally he must learn how to make a given movement and imitate others with precision, which is asking too much of a preschooler: just let him enjoy moving to music in his own free and exuberant way.

STEPPING ON YOUR TOES★ • Here is a game I played with my grandfather. The child puts one foot on each of your feet and then you both waltz around the room together. For an exciting finish, put some cushions on the floor and accidentally 'fall'.

★ This is especially good for children who can't walk or dance alone.

DANCE LIKE A BABY, WALK LIKE A GIANT ⭐ • Solo dancing at this age may simply consist of the child lying on the floor and kicking his legs to the music. Giant strides around the room to a slow march can be fun, or running on tiptoe to ballet music.

A QUICK BOB BEFORE BEDTIME • There is a time just before bedtime when the children are often silly or fractious. It is as if all their sensible bits are already asleep, and of course the last thing the awake bits will ever admit is 'I'm tired'. My eleven-year-old, in a desperate attempt to be allowed to stay up as late as possible, will still insist through stifled yawns that he is not a bit sleepy, even though his eyelids are slamming shut and his legs are buckling. One of the first signs of being really grown up and boring is that you cannot wait to be allowed to go to sleep, in my case usually as the main course is just finishing at a dinner party and I know I've still got to get through pudding and coffee and enough after-dinner conversation to avoid appearing rude.

One way to defuse the pre-bed tensions is to put on a tape or the radio, throw the cushions on the floor and let him dance and fall to his heart's content. It is a good filler whenever he has to wait – for lunch, for the rain to stop, when a friend is due.

Ring Games†

Ring games are part of the rich history of children's games which have been played in Europe – and elsewhere – for hundreds of years. The words and movements have passed through many generations of children (if a game is played between the ages of seven and ten, it passes through twenty-five generations every hundred years). If children didn't enjoy these games, they would have died out long ago. You need at least three children to play them, and rather more for games like 'The farmer's in the dell'.

'Ring-a-ring o' roses' is one of the simplest ring games. It is said to be about the Black Death – the 'roses' being flushed cheeks, the 'posies' handkerchiefs and the 'all fall down' self-explanatory.

⭐ If your child cannot control his own movements, rock, jiggle or kick his legs to different rhythms.

† Games with actions are good for children who find language difficult, because they communicate through signs, and actions can be interpreted as signs.

Ring-a-ring o' roses
Hold hands in a circle and walk round
A pocket full of posies.
Keep walking

A-tishoo! A-tishoo!
Mime sneezing
We all fall down.
And, of course, you do.

Other games to try are:

Here we go looby loo
Hold hands in a circle and move in to the middle
Here we go looby lie
Move out again
Here we go looby loo
Move in
All on a Saturday night.
Move out.

You put your left leg in
Stay in a wide circle and put your leg in towards the middle.
You put your left leg out
Stick your leg out behind you
You put your left leg in and you shake it all about
Shake your leg into the circle
You do the hokey kokey and you turn around
Let go of hands and turn around
That's what it's all about!

For 'The farmer's in the dell' the children form a ring with one child in the middle (the 'farmer'). They walk or skip around, singing, then the farmer chooses a 'wife', who joins him in the middle. The 'wife' chooses the 'child' and so on, until there are five children in the middle and everyone pats the 'bone'.

The farmer's in the dell
The farmer's in the dell
Hi ho the merry-o!
The farmer's in the dell

The farmer wants a wife, etc.
The wife wants a child, etc.
The child wants a dog, etc.
The dog wants a bone, etc.
We all pat the bone, etc.

NB: Verse three may be changed to 'The wife wants a career in media-based interactive technology' for those worried about sexual stereotyping.

Getting Ready to Read★

There are certain talents in children that inspire parental pride out of all proportion to their importance. This is particularly true with the first-born. Being potty-trained is a typical example. With my daughter I was ecstatically pleased with myself every time she managed to produce precious evidence of her brilliance into the pot, and deeply depressed and ashamed when she continued to wet nappies long after I felt she should have got the message. I took it all far too seriously and I think she enjoyed the power that gave her. One day after she had sat on the potty for ages, I taut and irritable and she stubbornly refusing to do anything, she finally got up and walked around the room, squatting now and then to spray a little damp patch every few inches until her supply was exhausted. The deliberate and

★ Most children who learn to communicate can be taught the rudiments of reading – it may just take longer, happen later and, inevitably, be harder to accomplish.

confrontational flouting of my authority was so funny that I burst out laughing, breaking not only my tension but also every rule about letting her know she could manipulate me so easily. From that moment on the tide turned and the potty-training progressed without a hitch. I've never forgotten the lesson.

Every stage of a child's development – sitting, walking, talking, recognizing shapes and so on – is a potential source of much exaggerated angst and pride. Reading is a particularly good example. Again, with my daughter, I thought I would be really clever and started her on Glen Doman flash cards at a very early age. Holding up a huge red-lettered 'daddy' in front of a tiny, gurgling baby has its silly side, but we both enjoyed it enormously, and I'm glad to remember I took it all with a very large pinch of salt. She did learn a few words extremely early, and it was a good parlour trick to impress the aunties, but I don't really think it had any effect whatsoever on her long-term reading ability.

As a general rule a child is not ready to read 'properly' until he can:

Speak fairly clearly, and use sentences
Understand and carry out simple instructions
Enjoy stories, and tell them to you
Remember and repeat songs and rhymes
Do simple jigsaws or other tasks which require the recognition of shapes and pictures
Play by himself.

Having a very young child who can read does not mean that child is especially clever, and it certainly does not reflect on *your* intelligence. Early reading should be something a child chooses, not something you force through your pride in parenting. Open the door by all means, but let the child walk through of his own accord.

Formal teaching is unnecessary and counter-productive at this age. Lay the groundwork for reading with games that make learning fun. Co-operation, tact and the readiness to abandon games before they become chores are essential. Too much pressure can teach your child that reading is an unpleasant, difficult and frustrating activity. Even if he cannot read a word before he starts school, he will have a head start if he loves books.

Reading begins with listening. Children who enjoy words are more likely to enjoy reading. Encourage your child to listen to the sound of words such as:

buzzing bees
hissing snakes
popping corks.

Teach him to delight in the sounds. Say it s-l-o-w-l-y. Say it quickly. Let your voice go down low and then raise it higher.

By the age of four, many children can begin to put things into sequences, understand what rhyming means and recognize letters and even words.

LONG WORDS • Encourage long words. 'Helicopter' was a favourite of my eldest, while my youngest enjoyed 'exaggerate' and 'distribution' – as well as most of the names of the dinosaurs. Why is this important? In order to read, children need to hear the little sounds that make up words, and to get the sounds in the right order. Long words encourage them to do this.

WHY? • At one time he always asked why; now it is your turn:

Why do you think that car is going so fast?
Why do you think that dog is barking?
Where did that squirrel go?
Can you see the dog in that picture?
Encourage him to talk and look.

RHYMES • Encourage him to hear rhymes. You can:

Read poems and stories in rhyming couplets
Make a deliberate mistake – it draws attention to the rhyme –
e.g. 'Humpty Davy sat on the wall'
What sounds like a cat? Mat and pat and sat. Take it in turns to find a rhyme
Which is the odd man out? Red, bed, dead, chair.
Make up a silly poem:

She sat on a seat
Combing her feet
The birds said, 'Tweet.
Bring us some meat'.

GETTING THE ORDER RIGHT • There are many ways to encourage your child to remember the order of things:

Give instructions: 'Go into the kitchen, look in the drawer by the sink and bring me a duster, please'

Tell him your plans: 'I'll finish the letter, then you can fetch me an envelope from the desk, you can stick on the stamp and then we will go out and post it'

Building and constructing (page 52) help him to plan. As do dressing, tidying up, putting clothes away, laying the table or sorting out the washing for you!

GOING FROM LEFT TO RIGHT • There is no logic to the way we read, we just happen to start each new line on the left and read to the right. To help 'stamp in' this order:

Put his clothes in a left to right order – pants on the left, trousers to the right and so on

Make a comic book: take a series of photographs of something happening in order – perhaps a trip to the shops or the park. The important point is that the sequence should be familiar. Arrange the photographs in comic-book fashion so that he reads them from left to right and from the top of the page to the bottom

Buy very simple children's comics to continue his 'training'.

FINDING THE PAIR • You can play this with jelly babies. Put a red jelly baby on the left and five others on the right, only one of which must be red. Can he find the pair? If you are trying to restrict sweet intake (good luck!), then try it with mugs, plastic animals, socks or letters.

LOOKING FOR STRANGERS • Put five ivy leaves in a row, plus one holly leaf. Can he find the stranger? You can make this task as easy or difficult as you like. Can he play it with letters?

MINE • Make a series of name cards: Mummy, Daddy, baby, goldfish and so on; include your child's name. Use them to mark places at the table,

to label washing as you sort it into piles, or on pegs in the hall. Let the child draw pictures of everyone in the family and put the labels under the pictures. If you have a daughter, keep the 'Mummy' label to use on your make-up, clothes and the car a few years later.

Words and Writing

Most children start to read by looking at a word and recognizing the pattern. It starts as guesswork. They look at the picture and 'read'. They will not recognize the word out of context; that needs practice.

Start by putting a few labels on some of the familiar things around your child – door, wardrobe, bed, cupboard. Choose words for their overall shape. Words such as house and drawer look different to us but the outline is similar: both start with a letter that sweeps above the line while all the other letters are short. Choose words with differing lengths which have the upward and downward strokes in different places, like bed and pillow. The more distinct they are, the easier he will find it to 'read' them.

For most children, reading starts with recognizing the shapes of whole words; knowing about letters and their sounds follows later. Much the same is true of writing. The triumphant achievement of being able to write their name can be a skill acquired much earlier than understanding the shapes of all the letters in the alphabet.

Children love to make marks on paper with coloured pens, and what they do with them seems to depend more on opportunity and interpretation than on age and intelligence. Most children start to write at the same time that they start to draw, but because we don't often recognize their squiggles as 'words', we are less likely to praise their efforts. We concentrate on the 'man', although he may look less like a man than those corner squiggles look like the written word. However, a line of squiggles captures the essence of writing: one shape follows another.

NAME CARDS   •   Once he has mastered a few words, you can begin to extend his vocabulary with word cards. Cut pictures from magazines, stick them to cards and clearly write what they are beneath the pictures in lower-case unjoined-up letters. Practise using them out of context.

TOYS TO BUY   •

Lotto cards and picture dominoes are great fun to play with and will help him to look for detail

Pairs or memory games will help him to remember positions and patterns

Puzzles which have words underneath will help to extend his vocabulary

And, of course, books – which is what it is all about

THE FIRST STORY ● Give your child some lined paper and ask him to write something for you. If he has seen you writing, he will probably make a few squiggles. Ask if you can keep what he has written and put it away carefully in a folder; let him see that it is important.

When a child who knows what writing looks like makes a line of squiggles, he recognizes what he has achieved. If he is praised, he will change and develop those squiggles until they look 'right' in exactly the same way that he changes and develops his drawing.

Drawing is one skill and writing another. He can do both independently, but he will often include a little 'writing' in his pictures. Ask him what he has written. He may not know – my son used to ask me to read them for him; he knew he could not read but was quite sure he could write.

I SEE A 'T'   •   In amongst his squiggles there is often something that looks like a 'real' letter, and a child who is familiar with letters may well see what he has written. Praise him and point out the lovely 'm', but be diplomatic; if he thinks only real letters are worth writing he may give up at this stage and that would be a pity. Telling your preschooler that only certain shapes are acceptable is a bit like telling him there is no point in drawing a man unless he puts all the fingers in the right place.

Now is the time to reinforce his skill by making the letters more familiar:

Look at road signs, house names and advertisements
Put magnetic letters on the fridge (we still have these in my house, used now mostly by the children in being inventive in creating rude words for each other)
Look at alphabet books
Can he find the letters of his own name? Is there a 'd' for Daddy?

Point it out when he has written an 'o' for orange or a 'j' for juice. Look for them the next time you are in the supermarket
Don't worry too much if he is mixing upper- and lower-case letters. Writing is a game, and at this stage he is simply discovering how to do it; later he will be formally taught. As he begins to 'know' his letters, he will start to change the squiggles to real writing.

PEN CONTROL • Once he starts school, a child will practise making letters by tracing outlines, which is fine once he sees other children carrying out the same task. He will know what he is aiming for: the most beautiful 'j' he can produce. But for a preschooler this sort of practice may well inhibit his spontaneous pleasure in writing. Let him develop hand control in a different context:

Can he join the two dots?
Can he follow the direction of the little arrows?
→ → →
← ← ←
Can he trace a wiggly line?
Can he draw around a template?
Can he draw inside a stencil?
Can he rip and fold paper? (See page 114)
Can he use scissors?
Can he undo a zip and fasten a button?
Can he colour between two lines?

FROM ONE LETTER TO ANOTHER • Draw attention to how letters are formed by asking him questions:

If he makes an 'r',
    can he turn it into an 'n'?
    and then an 'm'?
    or an 'h'?

If he makes an 'h',
    can he turn it into a 'k'?

LEARNING TO PRODUCE LETTERS • Usually the first letters a child learns to produce are those of his own name. If you write it on his drawings, he will soon learn how to do it. Sometimes he will write the letters in the wrong order (I wrote my name completely backwards for some time – no comments, please.) Don't worry – let them be. If he writes Majes instead of James, tell him how it sounds – he will correct it if he wants to.

Once underway, he may ask you for a few new letters or words. He might like you to write these for him to copy, or he may just want to look at what he can produce for himself.

SOME RULES ●

Give attention and praise – let him know you are interested
Answer questions
'Read' what he has written
Teach him if he asks; increase the opportunity to learn even if he does not
Help, but don't push.

WORKING TOGETHER ●

Let's make a shopping list
Let's write to Grandma
Let's write our cheques
Let's leave a message for Daddy to see when he comes in.

LEAVING MESSAGES ●   You can leave messages on the fridge:

Good morning
Have a good day
Buy eggs
I just can't cope any more
(only to be kept for special occasions).

Or in his bedroom:

Get up!
Brush your teeth
Pick up your toys.

NAMING LETTERS • Calling letters by names has little to do with writing, but it does help when he wants to use a letter and doesn't know how it looks, or if he wants to ask you how to spell a word. Some teachers believe in using sounds rather than the names of the letters, while others start with letter names. There is no right and wrong way; the children are unlikely to be confused by learning both, but you may want to follow the practice of his nursery school if he goes to one, or that of the local school he will be going to later. In my house we mostly used the sounds, but the names crept in occasionally too.

Yes it is Maths, But it's Fun!

It is easy to put children off maths for life by showing a dislike of it yourself, but to an unprejudiced child it can be made as much fun as anything else (or as tedious). Maths is the language in which scientists try to express the secrets of the universe, but it can be difficult to see its magic and fascination when tackling the boring business of learning tables or practising long division.

To a small child, numbers are just names. He may be able to sing out '1, 2, 3' like he sings out 'Jack and Jill', but to understand what they represent is more complicated.

> Understanding the concept of number is difficult because it is abstract. Ordering, matching and sorting objects helps your child to understand that concepts are ways of describing the relationship between one object and another: such ideas are fundamental to mathematics.

SOME WORDS OF EXPLANATION • You cannot point to a three, only to three things. We call a label that describes a group of things which have something in common a category. What three teapots and three socks have in common has nothing at all to do with any of the properties of a single sock or teapot; it has everything to do with how many objects there are. They share 'threeness'. One of a child's first tasks on the road to mathematical competence is to learn what the concept of number means.

We form lots of concepts: red, small, old, useful, ten. When your child starts school he will spend a lot of time looking for similarities between things – this is because he is being taught how to form concepts – but you can make a start now and help him on his way.

SORTING •   Sorting is simply seeing what two or more things have in common. Here are some simple sorting tasks:

Pairing up the odd socks
Sorting buttons into sets
Sorting out a mixture of different types of beans into groups:
haricot, butter beans, cannellini
Sorting the white washing from the coloured
Sorting his clean clothes from the pile of washing
Sorting knives, forks and spoons.

GIVING EVERY DOG A BONE • This is a little harder. The idea is to make sure that everyone ends up with the same things.

Lay the table giving everyone a knife, fork and spoon
Give every saucer a cup
Give every cake a cherry
Give everyone a drink.

ONE FOR YOU AND ONE FOR ME • Share out the sweets:

One for you
One for me
One for Daddy
One for teddy
One for this hand – that makes one
One for that hand – that makes one, two
One left over – that makes one, two, three.

Learning about numbers is learning how to match what you see or know against some standard. Once we can count and understand what numbers mean, the standard we use is the name we give to numbers. But how is a small child to understand this? When he chants '1, 2, 3', it is only a chant.

It is easiest for him to learn about numbers in the context of things he already knows. He has two hands. There are three bedrooms in his house and four people in his family.

Count out the picture cards – one for each person
Count out the gloves – one for each hand
Count out the covers – one for each bed.

Find as many examples as you can.

FAMILIES • Take a group of plastic farm animals:

Give every mummy a daddy
Give every couple a baby
Give them all a drink in the pond.

TOYS FOR MATCHING   •

Pairs (or Pelmanism as we called it when I was a child): Spread a pack of cards face down on a table or on the floor. Each player turns over two cards. If the pairs match – two threes, two queens, etc. – that player keeps them and has another go. The player with the most pairs wins.
Picture dominoes
Jigsaws – especially tray puzzles where he has to match the shape with a hole.

LINE UP   •   Draw pictures:

One hat
Two shoes
Three cats
Four balloons
Five cars.

Put them on the left side of the paper. If you can't draw and he thinks your cats are vacuum cleaners, then cut them out of magazines instead.

Write the numbers from 1 to 5 down the right side. Ask the child to pair up the pictures and the numbers. Can he do it when the numbers are in the wrong order? Draw lines in different colours from the objects to the correct numbers.

Fun with Art

Children are natural artists, and should be allowed to paint and draw as often as they like. When they are between about three and four years old, most children begin to draw things we can recognize: people and animals are favourite topics. Early drawings concentrate on what the child sees as important. People often have enormous hands because from the child's perspective they look that way as the adult reaches towards them to pick them up, to do up their buttons and so on. A cat viewed from the side may have a line of legs and a beaming front-facing smile. Don't discourage any

instinctive expression; even if his elephant looks more like a table, as long as he is pleased with it, then it *is* an elephant. ('Your people are far too tall and thin, Giacometti, I'm throwing the whole lot in the bin.') You should treasure these early masterpieces; there will come a time when he realizes his drawings are not 'realistic' and he will try to draw like a grown-up. Most artists spend much of their career trying to return to the innocent, uninhibited vision of their childhood.

Pencils for drawing should be large enough to hold comfortably and soft enough to make a mark without too much effort (nothing harder than an HB – a B may be better). Once a child is at the stage of knowing exactly what he wants his picture to look like, it is wise to have a rubber to hand in case things go wrong (you will have to use it for him; paper tears very easily when the rubbing-out is done by an inexperienced hand).

Painting takes time to set up and clear up afterwards, and the more elaborate the technique, the more preparation it needs. If you have only a few minutes to spare, there is really nothing to beat a clean sheet of paper and a few crayons or felt-tip pens. Do try to insist early on that all tops are replaced on felt tips – if left lying around uncapped they not only dry out, but they can also leak colour all over the furniture or bedclothes. Water-based pens are best.

Mix free-style drawing with painting, colouring and other techniques. Paint is messy, even if you have non-spill pots with a brush in each one, and it is hard for a child to control so you must expect spills – a waterproof sheet or moppable floor is a must. Gather everything together before you start, and stay on hand to deal with any major disasters. Protect the child as well as the floor and furniture; an old cotton shirt or a long-sleeved plastic apron is ideal.

Small children find it easier to work with thick paint. See page 85 for a paint recipe, or buy ready-mixed powder paint at good toy shops and art suppliers. Boxes of watercolour tablets are not really suitable for children of this age, who find it difficult to control how much water they use: they tend to end up with a box full of muddy-coloured liquid.

Although most people advise giving children only short, stubby brushes to use, you will find that your child will begin to get very frustrated without some finer ones too. I was always amazed at how neat my children could be if they were given the right tools, whereas the pictures they brought home from their nursery school were always of extremely chunky people with large blobby eyes – the only interpretation possible when working with a brush the size of your fist. Give him a choice of brushes, let him use fingers, cloths and small sponges too.

Non-tip pots make life easier, and putting a pebble in the base of each one makes them more stable. You will need one pot for each colour, with a brush in every pot if possible – much of the frustration small children experience when painting arises from attempts to wash brushes between colours.

Art is not just about creating pictures and free expression, it is about developing hand skills, pen control, co-ordination and careful observation. Do not be afraid to organize it. Even at this age art can be used to teach the child about planning, as common ground for conversation and to build confidence.

TO MAKE A NON-TIP POT • Choose a plastic soft-drink bottle with a neck wide enough to take a paint brush and cut it into three pieces as shown. Throw away the middle section. Put a pebble in the base. Invert

the top section, smear adhesive on the outer
surface just above the cut and
wedge it into the base.

ALL STUCK UP • Cutting and sticking are great fun, but a young child
can get very frustrated when his fingers won't keep up with his ideas and
things don't go as planned. Sitting with a pot of glue, scissors and a magazine,
my eldest son knew just what he wanted to do, but, after accidentally cutting
the carefully chosen racing car in half and getting glue on the wrong side
of the picture, he would throw everything on the floor. You will have to
be ready to give constant help and be very patient.

SNIP! • Half the joy of using scissors is cutting again and again, so why
make the whole thing complicated? Accept that scissors are difficult for

unskilled hands to use and discourage him from trying to cut around shapes until snipping is a well-practised skill. In any case, snipping is fun.

Provide a pair of safety scissors, a bowl to cut the bits into and some strips of paper. As he snips he will begin to learn to control the scissors. Strips 30 centimetres (12 inches) long and no more than 1 centimetre ($\frac{1}{2}$ inch) wide are easiest to handle, and a fairly heavy paper like writing paper is best. At first you will need to thread his fingers round the scissors.

You could help him stick his snipped bits on to a large sheet of paper in a collage to make him feel that he is working towards something rather than just cutting indiscriminately.

RIPPING • One of the problems a child faces when cutting things out is that he must use the skill of snipping while at the same time trying to direct the snips around pictures. It might be less frustrating at first if you teach him to rip. Start by simply ripping strips from pieces of paper, then make 'wiggly worms' by moving the paper as he rips it.

Once he can make worms, it is time to move on to more complicated shapes: circles, triangles, stars – even little men. When he has 'paper control', he can try to rip pictures from magazines, and when he has mastered that reasonably well it is time to start cutting out, by combining the snipping and ripping skills.

PAPER FOLDING • Another way to learn paper control is to start with very simple ideas: take a square of paper and show him how to bend it over, match the edges and press down the fold. Now fold it in half again – no more, or it will get too fiddly and stiff. Take a new piece of paper and do it again. Once he has mastered that, you can show him how to fold the paper diagonally.

SNOWFLAKES • Rip the corners off a twice-folded square of paper, open it out and you have made a simple snowflake. Once cutting is under control, he can try making snowflakes with scissors.

GLUE • Small children should not use adhesives, epoxy resins or wallpaper paste that has added fungicide. PVA (polyvinyl S acetate) is a non-toxic glue which can be sponged off most surfaces when newly applied. If it sticks to a jumper, put it in the freezer overnight and you can pick it off the next morning. Heat sets the glue, so washing the jumper in warm water will fix it permanently.

Home-made paste works well. Just add water to a handful of flour until it turns gooey, then add a pinch of salt.

Boiled paste makes a better texture: put 2oz/60g flour in a saucepan and add water until it makes a thin cream. Simmer the mixture for five minutes, stirring all the time. Add a little food colouring or glitter, and store the paste in the fridge in an airtight tin.

The food colouring or glitter helps to show where the glue is being spread, and it adds an attractive base colour to the finished work of art.

BRUSHES • Keep brushes just for sticking, as once they have been in the glue pot they are impossible to clean. Proper glue brushes are good, but spatulas are better for your children: they are easier to use, easier to clean and less wasteful.

SPREADING • Glue is difficult to spread on to tiny pieces of paper. It is better to spread glue on to a backing sheet and place or drop things on to the sticky surface. Choose a smallish piece of paper which is not too absorbent and help the child at first by putting a few blobs of coloured glue on to it and letting him spread them around as best he can with the spatula.

DROPPING • Once the glue is spread, he can drop a number of things on to the sticky surface. Here are some suggestions:

Rice, cracked wheat and other grains
Melon seeds, pumpkin seeds, dandelion seeds
Split peas, lentils and small beans
Oats, Rice Krispies and other cereals
Tea leaves and coffee grounds
Cocoa, drinking chocolate
Flower petals, leaves
Paper (including snipped and ripped bits)
Pieces of cloth and wool
Sequins, beads, buttons, cotton wool, glitter
Foil, milk bottle tops, polystyrene bits
Washed eggshell.

PASTING PROBLEMS • Once he can cut out and has got used to handling glue, you can show him how to paste the backs of his cut-outs, going right to the edges. It is easiest if you put the cut-out face down on to a spare piece of scrap paper and spread the glue on and over it. Change the scrap paper as often as possible or everything will get sticky on both sides.

TEMPLATE • A simple variation on the 'dropping' theme is to cover the backing paper in glue, put a template in position and scatter or drop decorations over the paper. When you lift the template away, the paper will be covered in glitter or lentils everywhere *except* where the template was. The child can fill this shape with a contrasting 'drop' if he wants to.

The template can be anything that covers the surface:

**A cup – good because he can lift it off easily
A shaped cake tin or jelly mould
Animal shapes
Large old puzzle pieces
Shapes you have cut from a card
Boxes, pots, rulers, rubbers, scissors.**

Draw a star shape on a large piece of stiff card. Cut out and remove the star without spoiling the area around it. Use the outer shape as a stencil. Put it on a sheet of paper. Give the child a brush full of glue and let him dab inside the star shape. Remove the stencil carefully and let him drop glitter or some other decoration on to the glued area.★ Shake off the excess to use again.

Use a gingerbread-man cutter to draw a shape on to card and make a stencil. Build up a picture by making a line of lentil, rice and cocoa people waiting for a bus. Use a straw for the bus stop.

STICKING BY NUMBERS   ●   This is a progression from the template theme. Draw a shape on to the paper, either freehand or by drawing round something like a cutter or a piece of a jigsaw puzzle. Glue inside the shape (this is where coloured glue is really helpful), then add the decoration to the glued area. Add more 'dropped' sections to build up a picture. A lovely Humpty Dumpty can be made, for example, by using bits of washed eggshell for his head, pieces of material for his trousers and a wall of torn pieces of brick-coloured paper.

Planned activities like this are important: they teach children to work towards an end and give you an opportunity of discussing with them why things have to be done in a certain order.

PRINTING   ●   Printing is another task which encourages the child to prepare and plan – underline this aspect by involving him in the preparation. Let him mix the paint and help you to cut up bits of string, chop carrots, collect leaves. Gather everything together and lay it out.

★ Children with limited or uncoordinated movement may find it easier to sprinkle using a sieve. If your child has a loose grip, put some lentils in his hand, move it towards the paper and help him let go.

Visually handicapped children will enjoy feeling the finished result of their pasting. Use more than one texture for the drops. You could also make a collage of dried herbs, petals and other materials impregnated with different scents.

MAKING A DIRECT PRINT •   Paint for the printing should be thick
– use the recipe on page 85. You can paint directly on to a washable table
or tray and then make a print by laying the paper over the painted area.
Press the paper down very evenly and roll over it with a paint roller or
rolling pin. Lift it up and there is your print.

   Printing is only really successful if the paper is absorbent; newspaper or
the back of wallpaper is ideal for first attempts.

PRINTING WITH OBJECTS •   You can use a wide range of objects as
printing heads. Use an ink pad or dip the object directly into paint or ink.
The first few prints may be of poor quality, but as you carry on the results
will improve as the coating on the head gets thinner. If your child is using
a small printing head, such as a carrot, make sure the paper is relatively small
too, or the process will become tedious.

Here are some good printing heads:*

Felt shapes
Parts of the body: fingers, hands, toes, elbows (and somebody is bound to suggest bottoms)
A soft rag, a cotton wool ball, foam, sponge, a scourer
Fruit cut in half, carrots, cabbage wedges, leaves
Cutting shapes from potatoes is traditional but turnips and swedes are more absorbent. Draw the shape on the cut side of the turnip, then cut around it. You should do this for a young child, but as he gets older he can manage as long as you are there to supervise
Initials cut into a rubber
Patterns of string stuck to blocks of wood – don't let any of the strings overlap
The edge of a ruler to make a line
Cotton reels
A matchbox
Wooden pegs.

Dressing Up

Much of the way we live our lives involves planning what we will do and what the effect will be by acting out possible scenarios in our heads. Imaginary games are a part of building this process; children have to learn what it means to be themselves, and what it means to be someone else. They are born with vivid imaginations and will naturally start pretending and 'being' other people with very little encouragement. Given one old hat, a child can see himself as the captain of the regiment or a space explorer, and even a vest pulled incompletely over the head and left dangling down the back can become a headdress.

Pretending to be someone else is the way the child learns what it is that makes each of us unique, and this includes learning that he is unique. Understanding another point of view – or even that another

*Select items for printing which you know children with limited movement and poor co-ordination can handle: potatoes which fit easily into the hand, leaves which can be dropped in the paint and then dropped on the paper. It will be more messy and you may have to guide hands, but the children will view the rather professional results of a printing session with pride.

point of view exists – does not really happen much before the age
of five. Games like these help.

A BOX OF CHARACTERS • Start a collection of dressing-up clothes. They needn't be special or in good condition – your local charity shop may be a useful place for picking up interesting bits and pieces, and throw in that disastrous dress you bought in the sales. At home, when I was a child, my mother kept a large assortment of old clothes in a dressing-up cupboard and my brother, sister and I would spend hours trying things on and changing into different characters.

MADE TO ORDER • It is easy to make special outfits very cheaply if you don't have to worry about them lasting for more than the length of a good game. You can sew the most marvellous costumes from lining material or calico, for example, and even crêpe or lavatory paper can be sewn and gathered if you treat it gently. Don't go for subtlety – use lots of bright colours, bits of glitter, beads and decoration – and staple, glue or safety pin rather than take the trouble to sew things on properly. Use paper doileys for lace (gold ones for princes and princesses), postcards stapled together for armour and sweets for jewels.

Teddies, Dolls and Other Little Worlds

Some children have imaginary friends, but most have pretend friends: dolls, soft toys and teddy bears. A teddy can play the dull parts in a game – or even *all* the other parts if there is no one else to play with. A teddy can be cuddled at night, or in the day when he needs a little confidence (the child, not the teddy – most teddies I've met have been remarkably self-confident and uncomplaining).

A pretend friend can also help a child to understand his own role in the adult world. The child is usually on the receiving end. His parents decide where everyone must sleep (and really he would prefer to be in Mummy's bed), what everyone eats, when he has to go to bed and even when he should go to the lavatory. But his teddy listens to *him*.

The child may not understand why parents are the way they are, but he can at least try to copy them. He can boss his teddies, leave them while he goes out, take them for a wee, bathe them, dress them and send them to bed early. He can be loving and gentle, mean and vicious, angry, caring or kind. He can have favourites and pick on others. He can be like us; and when we see ourselves in his games, it can be pretty horrifying.

Besides dolls and teddy bears, most children need a little world – a farm,

a doll's house, a battle station, a railway. The game is pretend, but the child doesn't take part; instead he stands outside and organizes the storyline, playing out his dreams and frustrations and the everyday happenings of his life.

Whether it is fashion dolls or battle figures, little worlds are almost always sex stereotyped. When small boys wanted to be engine drivers, train sets were very popular; now it is war machines and space battles for boys and pretty, sweet and glamorous dolls and animals for their sisters. Obviously there are exceptions and children will play with toys intended by the manufacturers for the opposite sex, but, from my own experience of watching my girl and two boys, there is no doubt in my mind that there is not much you can do to change the traditional leanings. I had all the usual good intentions of offering both sexes the same range of toys and books, but without any influencing they soon opted for the obvious male/female ones. You can try giving your son a pretty doll, but it will probably end up being used as a hammer or a battering ram. The great thing about teddies is that both boys and girls love to cuddle them.

Like books, toys are for sharing. There are common experiences which help even young children to communicate and play together. The sight of familiar toys reminds each child of games he plays with his parents or older children. Two children remembering similar games can play together even though neither of them can explain to the other exactly how to play the game.

BABY DOLL • The first baby doll is probably the only one you will ever choose, as later your children will develop strong ideas about which one they want you to buy. It is a good idea to purchase a doll with a soft, moveable body to start with. Not only is it more cuddly, but it is also much easier to dress than a stiff one. (If you have ever had a limb in plaster, you will remember how tricky it can be to manoeuvre ungiving arms or legs into narrow sleeves and trouser legs – dolls are just the same, and their owners can be a bit short on the necessary patience.) You will no doubt be called every few minutes to help put on or remove a little dress or jumper, but you might as well make the task as simple as possible for both of you.

DOLLS' FURNITURE   •   Small matchboxes can be used to make simple coffee tables or cradles. Cover them in cloth or sticky paper and glue them together in stacks to make a chest of drawers. Use just the sleeve sections stacked and glued together to make shelves, or stand them on end to form kitchen units; you could even cover the tops with Formica.

To make a wardrobe, cut down the centre of the outer box to make doors, then stand the box on its end. It is a good idea with all these pieces of furniture to glue them to a base to avoid the frustration of them falling over.

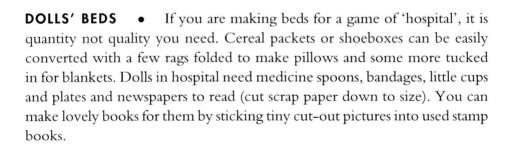

DOLLS' BEDS   •   If you are making beds for a game of 'hospital', it is quantity not quality you need. Cereal packets or shoeboxes can be easily converted with a few rags folded to make pillows and some more tucked in for blankets. Dolls in hospital need medicine spoons, bandages, little cups and plates and newspapers to read (cut scrap paper down to size). You can make lovely books for them by sticking tiny cut-out pictures into used stamp books.

TEDDY BEARS' PICNIC   •   Gather all the teddies (and I use the word in its loosest interpretation as a collective noun for anything with a personality – crocodiles, one-eared rabbits, broken dolls, a sock with paper eyes stuck on, Mummy). Put them on a rug in the garden (real, if you have one, or pretend). Give each guest a cup and saucer and a few teddy-sized sandwiches. Cut chocolate mini-rolls into slices, and add little cut-up pieces of apple, biscuit, cake and so on. You can make it a birthday party by adding a candle to one of the pieces of cake and dressing everyone in party hats and their best clothes. My daughter would play at these tea parties for hours, and a great deal of interesting imaginary conversation took place.

IF YOU NEED EXTRA FRIENDS • It is easy to make a few extra friends without going to too much trouble or expense. Paint a face on a wooden spoon and add a cloth skirt and plaited wool for arms.

Saw the bottom off an old-fashioned wooden clothes peg. Drill a hole just below the neck of the peg and thread a pipe cleaner through it to make arms, or simply twist the pipe cleaner around the neck. Draw or paint on a face and glue on wool, fur or shredded cloth for hair. Dress it in scraps of material.

You can make a Loet Vos doll as seen in the Museum of Childhood in Toronto. These dolls are very simple and extremely effective.

Fold a large square of cloth in half to make a crease, then roll each side in towards it. You should have a double scroll with a flat band in the middle. Now take a ball of cotton wool or small scrap of cloth and tuck it in the flat area between the two scrolls – about a third of the way down. Fold the top section over the ball and tie it in place to make the head. The rolls should be facing inwards, with the front section shorter than the back.

The front section forms the arms. Pull these into shape. Roll up the middle section and tuck it in. Loop a string around the neck, cross it over the front and tie it around the waist at the back. Tie more string around the 'wrists' to make hands. Draw on a face to finish the doll. You can cut the 'skirt' and tie the legs at the bottom to form a man.

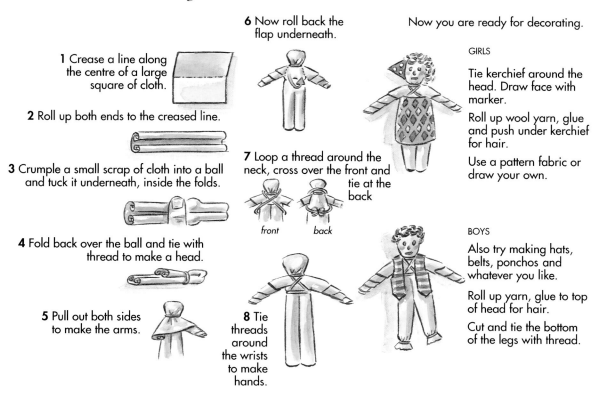

1 Crease a line along the centre of a large square of cloth.

2 Roll up both ends to the creased line.

3 Crumple a small scrap of cloth into a ball and tuck it underneath, inside the folds.

4 Fold back over the ball and tie with thread to make a head.

5 Pull out both sides to make the arms.

6 Now roll back the flap underneath.

7 Loop a thread around the neck, cross over the front and tie at the back

front   back

8 Tie threads around the wrists to make hands.

Now you are ready for decorating.

GIRLS

Tie kerchief around the head. Draw face with marker.

Roll up wool yarn, glue and push under kerchief for hair.

Use a pattern fabric or draw your own.

BOYS

Also try making hats, belts, ponchos and whatever you like.

Roll up yarn, glue to top of head for hair.

Cut and tie the bottom of the legs with thread.

CONCLUSION

Play remains an enjoyable and important part of our lives right through to old age (grandchildren are a great excuse to replay all those favourite childhood games). I have finished this book at the preschool stage not because that is the end of playing, but rather because its aspect changes gear once school starts and the whole concept of play becomes enmeshed in school and home activities.

On the other hand, I think it's important that children are never considered too old for silly games. Just as a three- or four-year-old loves the comforting feeling of pretending to be a baby every now and then, all children enjoy playing games just for their own sake occasionally, rather than always the more organized sports and 'educational' games in which they will become involved as they grow older. Many of the ideas in this book will continue to apply to older children, and the principles of playing for enjoyment and stimulation are just as relevant to a ten-year-old as to a two-year-old.

I do hope you have found this book useful and fun. If just one of the ideas in it has been responsible for raising one of those wonderful smiles from your baby, or just one game has produced an incapacitating and contagious fit of giggles in your toddler, it will have been more than worthwhile.

INDEX